NO MAMA, PAPA

*A gripping account of survival,
escape, rescue, and renewal*

SIDETH UNG

ISBN: 978-1-7169-3641-8 (sc)
ISBN: 978-1-7169-3640-1 (e)

Because of the dynamic nature of the Internet, any web addresses or links contained in this book may have changed since publication and may no longer be valid. The views expressed in this work are solely those of the author and do not necessarily reflect the views of the publisher, and the publisher hereby disclaims any responsibility for them.

Any people depicted in stock imagery provided by Getty Images are models, and such images are being used for illustrative purposes only. Certain stock imagery © Getty Images.

Lulu Publishing Services rev. date: 06/05/2020

Dedication

For Bryce, Sebastian, and Nikola Ung, without whom I would be void of the highest honor I know – that of being their father.

And because this is not my story alone, this book is also dedicated to my brother Sidan's children – Ricky, Randy, and Monica Ung, as well as my sister Sovannary's two boys – Tota and Keven Ung... and all our generations to follow.

Finally, I wish to extend this dedication to all those children who by God's grace will never know the unspeakable pain, suffering, and loss that your parents – my Cambodian brothers and sisters – saw firsthand. Their story is told here too, for you.

Acknowledgements

First and foremost, I wish to offer my heartfelt love and gratitude, as well as the highest respect possible, to my older sister and brother – Sovannary Ung and Sidan Ung – as well as each dear member of our family who lost their life under the tyranny of Pol Pot and his Khmer Rouge regime. Without their struggle to live and their abiding love for me, I would not be here. Their sacrifices will not go untold.

Words fail to express the gratitude I feel for my foster Cambodian father and mother, *Père* and *Mère*. On multiple occasions they risked their own lives and even the safety of their household to save Sovannary, Sidan, and more often me. Christ said that the greatest love of all is when one is willing to give their life to save another. For this reason, Père will forever live in my heart as the greatest hero I have ever known.

This same degree of gratitude and respect extends to my Aunt Sim Long, my Uncle Kari Mam, and all my wonderful Mam family cousins who opened their hearts and home to Sidan and me when we had no other family and nowhere to go. I am particularly grateful for the fierce, sacrificial love and devotion Aunt Sim demonstrated for me and my rescue. And beyond that, for her daughter, Malis, who became a surrogate mother to me – making sure I was fed, bathed, and happy during those days of transitioning to America and getting settled in.

A special thanks and highest regard are due Jerry and Libby Percifield, our sponsors to America, as well as to the Catholic Foundation and the Catholic Relief Services. Without their help, none of this would have been possible.

Words cannot convey the depth of my love and gratitude for Jim and Regina Hughes, my American dad and mom, as well as for Aunt Athelia and Uncle Don Jordan, and Papa and Nanny Woodard – all who welcomed me with open arms and hearts into their family as one of their own. They taught me the beauty of love over hate. They showed me God. They taught me how to live well and keep evil at bay. They gave me the priceless gift of wonderful, warm memories with extended family and allowed me the opportunity to fully experience the childhood I missed out on earlier in life.

Finally, I am deeply grateful for the unbreakable bond I share with my adopted brother and sister, Peter and Sarah Hughes and their families, as well as those wonderful cousins I inherited in Jonathan and Don Jordan. From the moment I first entered their world at the age of eight, they seamlessly and abundantly filled the void that was left when my blood kin were brutally taken from me. These dear people took me in, kept me close, and never let go. They made certain I felt what they were conveying – that I was their "brother from another mother."

You all are stars that gave me light and hope. You all are priceless, irreplaceable treasures in my heart and in my life.

My prayer is twofold: that you know my unending love and gratitude for you… and that I never, ever disappoint you.

On a different note, it is amazing how God brings people in and out of your life for one purpose or another. One such individual – Larry Marcinko – was at one time a co-worker of mine. In the course of conversation, Larry discovered enough about my story to move him to urge me to tell it. At that point in my life, however, I was more interested in forgetting those horrors than remembering them.

But Larry gently persisted. And thus began a relationship that spawned the very first draft of the book you now hold in your hands. For Larry's undying enthusiasm and untiring efforts, I will be forever grateful as he was, at least from my limited perspective, the spark that lit the fire of my passion to share this intimate and most difficult of times with you.

Contents

PART 3

Preface

To be honest, I have mixed feelings about sharing my story. Part of me would rather not, for several reasons.

First, I have no desire to revisit those heart-wrenching events that define my past. The learned ability to block traumatic scenes and horrific memories from one's own mind is an essential tool for survivors like me. In fact, decades passed before I ever gave those dark years of my life a second thought – and before committing to this project.

Also, publicly exposing your raw pain and devastating losses creates feelings of vulnerability. You never know how people will see you after they know that part of your journey. Maybe they will pity you. Maybe they will think of you as a second-class citizen. I understand these are possible outcomes of telling my story.

Further, I do not want sympathy, or pity, or any kind of special attention for any misfortune I have experienced (probably because it reminds me of that time in my life when standing out from the crowd got you shot). I prefer to blend in as just another American.

And yet, the older I get the more I am convinced that I must tell my story. As devastating as these experiences were, they are chapters in my life. *They are the foundational part of my reality.* Everything I went through contributes to the person I am today, and that includes the years and experiences in Cambodia. If I deny these memories their right to be heard, I will miss out on whatever role they serve, for they are as much a part of me as my skin.

These events happened to me when I was a young boy. I now have boys of my own… and words can never express how thankful I am that my boys will never experience the pain I knew as a child.

At the same time, I want them to understand how precious life is. I want them to appreciate the freedoms we have – the freedom we have to live and *be*. I want to tell my story for them, as it is their heritage and a true source of strength and inspiration they can draw on as they grow older.

If you know anything about the travesties Cambodians suffered under Pol Pot's communist regime from 1975 to 1979, you know that my story is representative of the stories of many, many other dear people who survived. They too, lost much. I tell my story to honor them, as well as to speak for those millions whose voices were silenced by the murderous, evil Khmer Rouge.

And I must tell you that although painful, the completion of this project has been good for me personally. If I have learned anything, it is this: that life does not simply consist of circumstances. Rather, life is the opportunity you and I have to take our circumstances and make something beautiful out of them.

I realize I have been given much. Much pain and sorrow, to be sure. But through it all – and *beyond* it all – I have been blessed more than I have ever suffered. You will meet many wonderful, caring, selfless people in the pages that follow, people who showed up in my life at just the right time and place. They made all the difference, and I would not be where I am or who I am without them.

In closing, I am in awe of how my life has been preserved. I narrowly escaped death on numerous occasions. So I am grateful to just be alive. I am grateful for the God who brought me safely here and I have to believe it was for reasons beyond what I can ever know, even bigger than all the reasons I have mentioned.

This is why I tell my story.
I wish you peace,

Introduction

I was born in 1972, so the fuel of revolution that would soon turn my beloved country into an inferno was already ignited by the time of my birth. Couple that with the fact that my earliest memories start showing up around age three or four, and you understand why much of my early story is gleaned from older siblings and cousins.

But whether from a compilation of the memories of others or my own, the story you are about to read is not embellished or exaggerated in any way. It is shared, as much as is humanly possible, in its truest, purest form.

And since different aspects of my story often play out on various stages, when those family members integral to the story are sharing from their vantage point, it is given in their own words. In the text I have made the reader aware when someone other than myself is speaking.

Early in the book I also include a synopsis of the geographical and political history of my country. There are two reasons for this. For one, it helps to understand the context in which the story takes place. My other reason is that I want to aid the reader in better understanding the players driving such horrific, bizarre, and irrational events. Once that backdrop is set however, the story reverts from political and historical to personal.

When I first set out to write my story, I planned to end the book with my arrival in America. But because so many of the challenges – and blessings – in my life happened post Cambodia, there was just so much more to tell. So the significant events from those early years are presented in this book as well.

PART 1

1

Caught in the Middle

I am one of those people to whom family means everything. As my story unfolds, I think you will understand why. For you see, not just once, but on multiple occasions different members of my family risked their own life to save mine.

Another reason I am so passionate about family is because I was fortunate enough to be blessed with not just one – but *four* loving, supportive families by the time I reached third grade. Maybe that explains in part how I survived when so many others became casualties of a horrible and senseless war. I am living proof that *"no man is an island."*

My Cambodian family – that is, my biological family – was quite large by American standards. There were ten of us in all…

My dad, Neak Ung, born in 1934

My mom, Kim Sorng Long, born in 1944

An older sister, Sovannary, born in 1960

An older sister, Sotheavy, born in 1962

An older brother, Sidan (birth name Sokha), born in 1964

An older brother, Ratanavuth, born in 1966

An older brother, Maliane, born in 1967

Yours truly, Sideth (birth name Sokphadeth), born in 1972

A younger sister, Sovannara, born in 1973

A younger brother, Phoenix Ruessei, born in 1976

In order to set the background for you, it is important that you get to know my first family – my family of origin – as it was before I was born.

My dad and mom and older siblings originally lived in one of the largest cities in the Takeo Province of Cambodia, located about 50 kilometers, or 31 miles, from the border with Vietnam. (The southernmost boundary of the Takeo Province borders what was then South Vietnam.)

Both my dad and paternal grandfather were well educated men, allowing them to hold prominent positions in government. My dad worked for the Cambodian federal government. He headed up the Immigration Department. My paternal grandfather was a local official, similar to a mayor.

As a result of Dad's position, my family enjoyed an upper-middle-class lifestyle in Takeo. They had a nice, large home in the city for their growing family. It had both marble and hardwood flooring, a tile roof, a large front porch, and a spacious backyard.

Mom loved her home and took great pleasure in her role as housewife. Though Dad employed maids and nannies to help with the children and the chores, Mom insisted on doing most of the housework because she prided herself in keeping her home orderly and clean. In that wonderfully endearing British expression, Mom was *house proud*. In fact, she once cleaned the hardwood floor until it was as shiny as glass. Unfortunately, it was also slippery as ice. When Dad came home from work later that day, his feet slipped across that slick floor and he fell on his rump!

My family's idyllic life in Takeo Province comes to an end in late 1970 when both the Vietnam War and the growing civil war in Cambodia begin escalating.

As the fighting penetrates deeper into Takeo Province, Dad moves the family about 50 miles north to Phnom Penh, the capital city of Cambodia. He believes this area is far enough away from the fighting that the family will be safe here.

The house in Phnom Penh is a good bit smaller than the one they left behind. But they determine to make the best of it, since they only plan to stay here temporarily.

I was born a little more than a year after the move to Phnom Penh.

Because my closest sibling is already five years old when I arrive, I become known as *Mom's little shadow*. And since I am the baby of such a large family (at least for now), I can only imagine how much I was doted on.

But by the time of my birth, the Vietnam War is escalating in intensity and Cambodia is quickly becoming the battleground of choice. Though no one recognizes it, all the pieces of the puzzle which will forever alter our world are already in place. Life for my family will *never again* be normal.

This fact explains why, as I will be sharing with you, I do not remember any of my siblings, save for my older brother Sidan. I have only one or two vague memories of Mom and Dad. I desperately want to remember them. And I have tried.

But being so young when I lost most of my biological family means I have no facial recall of them at all. To put it succinctly, I don't even know what my parents and all but two of my siblings looked like. As a result, my memory of family is simply a general sense of how it felt to be with them.

Everyone who knew her says that my mom was very beautiful. Graceful in spirit, she was gentle, soft-spoken, and calm. Two of my earliest memories that I treasure with all my heart involve Mom and me.

I remember helping Mom clean vegetables, especially ones that were long and green. I assume those must have been a type of celery that she used in her fish soup – one of my favorite dishes.

But this next memory is my favorite. As the family gathers on the floor around the dinner table one evening, instead of sitting upright I decide to lie on my side to eat. I guess I thought that would be cool. I remember Mom telling me that I should not lie down and eat, or I would turn into an alligator. Seeing as I hated alligators, I never tried that again!

Not only was I blessed to be born into a loving family, I am proud to say that my homeland of Cambodia is also quite naturally beautiful. This Southeast Asian country shares borders with Thailand to the northwest and west, Laos to the north and northeast, Vietnam to the east and southeast and the Gulf of Thailand to the south.

Contributing to Cambodia's beautiful landscape are large lakes and rivers, lush central plains, dense jungles, towering mountains, and warm gulf waters.

In addition to her physical beauty, Cambodia historically enjoyed political power and prominence. Modern Cambodia's predecessor, the ancient Angkor Empire (also known as Kambuja), dates back to 802 A.D.

Massive, majestic temples still stand today in what was once the Empire's capital city of Angkor. These ruins speak to Cambodia's immense power and wealth, impressive art and culture, and architectural achievements and expertise in times past. In fact, satellite imaging shows that during the 11th to 13th centuries, Angkor was the largest preindustrial urban center in the entire world! This is a rich heritage indeed.

Fast forward to 1863, when France made Cambodia a protectorate, naming it "Cambodje." (A protectorate is a dependent territory that enjoys local autonomy while maintaining certain obligations to its sovereign state.) During this period of Cambodia's history, France established universities and industries in the cities that gave great benefit to its citizens. These establishments also introduced a Western feel to the cities of Cambodia.

Cambodia was eventually granted self-rule within the French Indochina Union until 1946, and later gained full independence in 1953.

The 1950s and early 1960s were a golden age for Cambodia. In 1960, the last king of Cambodia died and his son, Prince Sihanouk, took over as chief of state. During this time 90 percent of peasants owned their land. The country prospered. Rice and fish – staples in Asia Minor – were abundant. More importantly, unlike her neighboring countries of Laos and Vietnam, Cambodia was at peace.

But Prince Sihanouk could not prevent what he most feared – that the civil war going on between North and South Vietnam would spread across Cambodia's borders. He was concerned that his country's neutrality made Cambodia a safe zone for Vietnamese communists to establish base operations. As it turns out, he was more right than he could have ever imagined.

American forces began bombing North Vietnam heavily in 1965. When that happened, North Vietnam started moving soldiers and equipment into Cambodia and setting up bases and sanctuaries there as part of their battle strategy.

As a result, in 1969 America's newly-elected President Nixon secretly ordered strategic bombing of the North Vietnamese and Viet Cong sanctuaries in Cambodia. Unfortunately for the locals, this only served to drive these Vietnamese communists deeper into our country – and communism itself into the hearts of many of our rural citizens, at least for a while.

Spillover from the Vietnam War was not the only problem facing Cambodia, however. Internal problems began brewing inside the country as well. Peasant farmers complained of corruption and unfair treatment from the government. These actions created unrest, which played perfectly into the hands of the small but growing underground communist movement in Cambodia – the Khmer Rouge.

In March 1970, while Prince Sihanouk was out of the country, large-scale anti-Vietnamese demonstrations erupted in the capital city of Phnom Penh. The escalation of this tension resulted in a military coup which ousted Sihanouk (who was politically sympathetic to North Vietnam) from power. One of his right-wing generals, Lon Nol took over. General Nol was a supporter of the South Vietnam/U.S. cause.

April 30, 1970, turned out to be a crucial date for my country. On that day, President Nixon announced that American and South Vietnamese troops were officially taking the war into Cambodia to stop the army of North Vietnam and their Viet Cong allies. This decision threw my country further into chaos.

What resulted from that announcement surprises most people, unless they are students of the Vietnam War. For the next five years the U.S. military dropped *three times* as much bomb tonnage on Cambodia as they did on Japan in World War II! It goes without saying that in the process they also took the lives of hundreds of thousands of Cambodians.

All the while, communist-backed guerillas of the Khmer Rouge continued to organize forces in the jungles. And though America's stated purpose for the Vietnam War was to stop communism, the bombing campaigns had exactly the opposite effect in Cambodia. U.S. bombing efforts provided easy fodder for the Khmer Rouge to use in their recruiting propaganda. The following reality proves this point.

In 1969, Khmer Rouge forces numbered about 10,000. After four years of intense bombing by the U.S., their number of recruits ballooned to over 200,000! Other factors were in play that helped contribute to such widespread support, of course. But the years of devastation and death caused by the U.S. bombing was the single biggest reason the Khmer Rouge guerilla forces grew so rapidly.

As they gained power, the Khmer Rouge began methodically moving into the cities with a focused purpose. Their central mission was to dismantle the infrastructure of modern Cambodian society. They also infiltrated the countryside, taking control of all the agriculture. Overnight, individuals no longer owned their land or the crops they grew. Under the command of their near faceless leader Pol Pot, *by 1973 the Khmer Rouge had seized control of almost 85 percent of our nation's land.*

It was during this turbulent time that I was born. Not only had the Vietnam War moved well into Cambodia by then, the country was also on the brink of its own civil war.

This explains why after being in Phnom Penh less than two years, Dad decided we needed to move again. My dad was a wise man with smart, solid connections. He understood a lot of what was going on in our country and where we were likely headed, and he was trying to stay one step ahead.

This time we move 80 miles northwest to Battambang, the capital of Battambang Province and the second largest city in Cambodia. Battambang is the safest province at the time. It is much closer to the border of Thailand and thus that much farther from Vietnam. This is in 1973.

Thankfully, there is much less fighting going on in Battambang. It seems we have moved far enough away from the bombing, chaos, and conflict that we are finally safe. I imagine in the back of Dad's mind he wants us to be able to stay here long enough for the wars – both the Vietnam War and Cambodia's own civil war – to dissipate. Hopefully then we can return to our beloved home in Takeo Province.

The Vietnam War officially ended in 1975. At that point the Americans pull out of Vietnam as well as Cambodia. People are ecstatic that the war has ended, and the bombing has stopped. It looks as if life can now get back to normal.

What Cambodians, and indeed the rest of the informed world do not realize however, is how much worse the post-war tsunami will prove to be. Our people, including my mom and dad, have no idea what is coming. Had my parents known we were headed into the darkest hour in the history of our proud land, we would never have stayed in Cambodia.

2

A Dreadful Journey

If you have never lived in the eye of war… never heard the screams that follow the ongoing explosions… never felt the gut-wrenching grip of fear and dread of knowing that you and your family could be the next casualties… you cannot relate to how awful war really is. Shells indiscriminately fall from the sky, peppering our country in both densely and sparsely populated areas. If you run from the city in order to escape, the next thing you know they are falling in the countryside. It is maddening.

My people suffered horrific physical injuries, loss, and death as a result of the U.S. bombing campaign in Cambodia from 1965 to 1973. But the severe psychological repercussions may have been even more difficult. Existence was reduced to a state of constant terror and confusion. Life began to consist of nothing more than just trying to stay alive.

This is the setting in which the Khmer Rouge army, under the command of the devious and sinister butcher Pol Pot, begins gaining control. The U.S. bombing efforts supply all the energy the *Rouge* need to fuel their propaganda campaigns, allowing them to convert many of the Cambodian people into revolutionaries with relative ease.

To better understand what drove the Khmer Rouge army to power, let's look at where they came from… starting with the name Khmer Rouge. Khmer refers to the Khmer people – an ethnic group that includes mostly

Cambodians – as well as for the native language itself. Just as the British speak English, the native Cambodians speak Khmer.

And *rouge* is a holdover from the French influence. *Rouge* is the French word for red.

So why red? Because communists have traditionally chosen red as their representative color. You may know that the armed forces of the Communist Party of China from 1928 to 1937 were known as the Red Army. And the Russian Soviet army created by the communist government after the Bolshevik Revolution of 1917 were also called the Red Army.

So Khmer Rouge means "the Red Khmers," that is, the communist Khmers. More specifically, the Khmer Rouge are the communists in Cambodia aligned with Pol Pot and his bloodthirsty regime.

Pol Pot's mission was to socially engineer a classless communist society. He believed simple village life to be communism in its purest form, so he set out to erase all traces of the modern world. He determined that cities were evil and devised a plan to force all those who lived in the cities into the countryside in order to build a shared agrarian society. Basically, he wanted to take Cambodia back to the stone age.

Pol Pot was as evil as he was morally insane. One of his well-known… and rigorously practiced beliefs was, *"Better to kill an innocent by mistake, than spare an enemy by mistake."*

Ironically, Pol Pot was well educated. He taught history, geography, and French literature at a private school for seven years. That was his public life. And yet all the while he was employed by the school system, he worked diligently in the evenings plotting his revolution. Surrounded by carefully chosen, like-minded *comrades*, he organized an intricate plan to overthrow Lon Nol's government and convert Cambodia to communism.

His political platform identified intellectuals, residents of the cities, ethnic Vietnamese, religious leaders, and civil servants all as *enemies*. This explains why the Khmer Rouge focused on recruiting the indigenous country people, the uneducated, and disadvantaged farmers, to join the revolution. And because of everything they had suffered to date (victims of a Vietnam war they did not sign up for), the Khmer people did not question Pol Pot's mission. Understandably, they were thrilled with the prospect of revenge.

So when Pol Pot's rebels began moving into the villages and coun-tryside, the farmers were ready to give them whatever they wanted. In exchange for their land, tools, and food, the communists put guns in their hands and organized them around a cause. They convinced them to turn over their belongings for the good of the uneducated masses in exchange for the chance to fight back with force. They systematically brainwashed them.

That's how the Khmer Rouge grew so rapidly. In large part, these Khmer Rouge were the "have-nots" who had suffered tragedy, loss, and devastation as a result of the Vietnam War. Pol Pot's loyalists offered them hope and a way to finally stand up to their "oppressors." It would soon be all too obvious that this was a *false* hope.

This was no typical coup – a case of the Khmer Rouge opposing the Cambodian government and wanting to overthrow them so they could take over politically. Rather, a deep-seated, primal hatred was energeti-cally at work, stoking the fire of an unstoppable and catastrophic killing machine.

History proves conclusively that an evil individual or movement with conviction is a danger. Add to that cocktail immense power and you have the makings of a maniacal despot. Like Pol Pot. A statement of his shows what I mean: *"He who protests is an enemy. He who opposes is a corpse."*

By the early 1970's, these communist rebels were a deadly, but still fairly secretive, army that had quickly grown from about 10,000 to over 200,000. And yet their leaders remained completely unknown to the out-side world. This was even true of their undisputed head, the 47-year-old Pol Pot.

What's more, America's political decisionmakers wrongly assumed that the Khmer Rouge was controlled by the Viet Cong. So when President Nixon announced to the world on January 23, 1973, that an accord had been reached to end the Vietnam War, the U.S. was sure the cease fire would apply to Cambodia as well. All the while however, an enemy the ill-informed Nixon never imagined grew larger and stronger by the day.

April 16, 1975, marked a dreadful moment in Cambodia's history. On this day U.S. Marines were ordered to evacuate their embassy in the capital city. As America's involvement in the war was all that had been keeping

Lon Nol's weak anti-communist government alive, her decision to withdraw troops led to the immediate destabilization of Lon Nol's fledgling army. Without U.S. support, they could not sustain.

Basically, the world had just abandoned Cambodia to its fate. In her attempt to "end" the war, the U.S. opened the door for the now powerful and vicious Khmer Rouge. This act was the green light for these guerillas to officially begin their mission to destroy – and then reorder – Cambodian society, murdering more than two million Cambodians in the doing.

At dawn on April 17, 1975, Khmer Rouge soldiers enter the capital city of Phnom Penh. Initially there is a sense of hope that *"the war has ended!"*

Citizens are celebrating in the streets, streaming white sheets out of their apartment windows, and putting flowers in the barrels of the soldiers' guns. Shouts of *"peace is here!"* echo up and down the streets of the city.

But this short-lived celebration abruptly turns to chaos when Pol Pot's troops begin randomly firing shots in the air and shouting angry threats. The people are forced to leave under the ruse that the Americans are about to bomb the capital. *"If you want to survive you must leave Phnom Penh!"*

This is pure propaganda, of course, but since the U.S. had dropped so many bombs already, it is an easy sell. The people are in panic mode. They have no idea what to believe.

The Khmer Rouge make it easy to decide. If you choose not to follow orders, you are shot. Imagine how confusing this must have been – to be told you must leave in order to survive, but then be forced to do so at gunpoint!

No one saw this coming. Residents of the city had no warning, and no time to prepare. So of course, everyone begins quickly gathering their families and packing what supplies they can throw together for a few days. Dried meat, rice, pickled and dried vegetables, any food that will travel is quickly collected. They hurriedly grab clothes, money, jewelry, and whatever other important belongings they can put in a sack.

Every last one of Phnom Penh's two million citizens – even those who are sick and dying – are ordered to flee to the countryside. Anyone who resists is shot on the spot.

Twenty-four years after joining the communist party, Pol Pot's dream of a revolution begins unfolding before his eyes. From his vantage point, his vision of *utopia* is finally becoming a reality.

Within days of the Khmer Rouge's overthrow of Lon Nol's government, the formerly bustling, densely populated capital city of Phnom Penh is nothing more than a ghost town.

The Vietnam War that Cambodia is unwillingly sucked into has ended. The civil war between Lon Nol and the Khmer Rouge, over. The incessant bombings have stopped. But mass and brutal starvation and slaughter lie ahead.

The specter of Death hangs like a black cloud over my country. My people are unknowingly headed into what many historians believe is *one of the most barbaric and murderous periods ever in the history of the world.* (By the time the Khmer Rouge is brought down, almost 25% of Cambodia's 1975 population will have perished because of them.)

If you remember, my dad was afraid something like this would happen. That is why he moved our family 180 miles northwest of Phnom Penh to Battambang a couple of years earlier.

I am three years old at this time, and my earliest memories are starting to kick in. So I can personally remember a good bit of what is about to happen.

Less than a year after the assault on Phnom Penh, we look out the windows of our home in Battambang to see the Khmer Rouge now patrolling the streets of our town too. Needless to say, we are terrified.

I still get a sense of fear and feel a primal need to run when I think about it. It is as if I am right there again, seeing it for the first time. Young, angry, dark-skinned men in black pants, long-sleeved black shirts, and red-and-white checkered scarves tied around their foreheads are everywhere. They fill the streets. Some are walking around, others are sitting or standing in the backs of the trucks that are moving slowly up and down the main street of the city. And they all have rifles.

Just as they did in Phnom Penh, they yell threats into their bullhorns, telling everyone to pack and leave their homes because the Americans are about to bomb the city. They give orders for all shops to be closed and all weapons to be turned over to them.

While this is going on, somebody knocks on our door. When Dad opens the door, two of these men are standing there. Two very tall, stone-faced soldiers wearing the same kit – black pants, long-sleeved black shirts, and long red-and-white checkered scarves. And carrying guns. Always the guns.

They never aim their weapons at my parents. But they talk to them. And while they are talking, we kids all cower in corners farther back in the house.

I see their faces, like chiseled stone shaped into a scowl, and their eyes, their hate-filled eyes. God help you if they see you… if those fiery eyes look at *you*.

When they finish talking, they go. And then my parents tell us we must pack and leave our home. Everyone seems to understand there is no negotiating the order. My older siblings pitch in to help Mom and Dad get what they think we will need.

By this time my family has already moved twice as a result of this war – once from Takeo Province to Phnom Penh and then later from Phnom Penh to Battambang.

But this move is different. This time we are *forced* to move – not because of what Dad feared was coming but because of what is now *here*.

Our worst nightmare has happened; the Khmer Rouge have caught up to us. We are no longer one step ahead.

Why did these men not kill my father right then and there? As a former government official, his name is certainly on their most-wanted list. The Khmer Rouge know who he is.

I think it is because they have no immediate reason to kill you unless you choose to disobey their orders to leave. They are in charge now, and thus, in no hurry. Besides, their tactics are a lot more sinister than that. For the time being they need us. Or should I say, *they have plans for us.*

All the while, they are busy identifying anyone with any type of education or even association with the educated class of people. Not only that, if you wear westernized clothing… or glasses (indicating you can read)… if you are a teacher… if you hold a position of leadership in the government… or even if you just *sound* educated, the kiss of death is on your head. Even lighter-colored skin can indict you because the darker your skin, the more likely you are to be indigenous, or to work in the sun, and not be part of the educated class.

If you match any of these criteria, it is simply a matter of time before the Khmer Rouge find you and kill you. So obviously, my dad's name is on their list. The Khmer Rouge know about him.

While the older family members busily pack our belongings, I watch out the window to take in what is happening outside. The soldiers continue yelling threats, *"Leave before the Americans bomb the city. Hurry… leave the city! Take as little as you can! You must leave now!"*

I watch as people run frantically about, gathering their families and loading up what they can carry in cloth bags or sacks. All the while, the soldiers wave their guns above their heads and periodically fire random shots into the air. No one dares to resist because remember, in Pol Pot's mind, to resist means you are an enemy. *Their message is clear… and their threats are real.*

Some people leave in cars, others on motorbikes, and still others on bicycles. But most people, like my family, go on foot. Dad decides we should walk – a horrible idea from our perspective as children, but less horrible than announcing that you are a "have." You do not want to look like you belong to the *haves* – those with wealth, education, and status.

Besides, those with modes of transportation only have them until one of the soldiers says, "Give me your car," or "Give me your bike." And that's that. Whatever they want, they take. (For that matter, they're just as likely to say, "Give me your hat.")

We all inch along as one huge mass leaving the city. The soldiers take us down the main road to a narrow paved road, and eventually onto this dirt road. Out of the city and into the country we go. No one has any idea where we are going. We are simply following because we have no other choice.

Imagine what a strange, senseless, and bizarre scene this is. A massive band of people – some on wheels and some on foot – moving as one down the dirt road. You hear parents continually urging their children to hold each other's hand so they can stay together and not get lost in the crowd. Soldiers randomly shout threats and fire shots in the air if some lag behind. And every time this happens the panic, pushing, and shoving get a lot worse.

Those who are stronger can keep up. The younger and weaker ones struggle. *But no one stops.* No one quits because soldiers line the perimeters of the crowd on every side of us.

Every now and again babies cry, and children complain to their parents of being tired or hungry. You hear pots and pans clanging and countless pairs of feet shuffling along the road. But hardly anyone talks. We just keep moving – one giant mass being herded to... who knows where.

At some point on the journey everyone starts running, but I have no idea why we have to run or what we are running from... or to. We don't even know *that* basic fact. My older brother Sidan just tells me to run. But I can't keep up, so Sidan ends up carrying me.

While we are running, I hear loud explosions and gunfire. A lot of gunfire. Somehow in the middle of all the confusion I get hit with shrapnel in my right leg. Blood is running down my leg and off the bottom of my bare foot. But I don't even cry because there is so much chaos and craziness that even if I did, no one would hear me.

The best I can tell is that in the middle of all this madness, part of the crowd is wanting to kill the other part. And the people who don't wish to harm *anyone* are running from those who want to kill *everyone*. As you can imagine, panic abounds. You might be shot at from one direction one minute and a completely different direction the next.

Because I don't understand any of this, all I know is that I feel a strong sense of loss – loss of what makes sense, loss of family, loss of home, loss of safety and security, loss of everything we once had. It feels like something is being ripped out of me. It's all wrong and makes me feel sick to my stomach.

It's *everywhere.* I just want to be safe. I just want to get away from everything that is going on right now.

But where to? And how do you get there?

At some point the explosions and gunshots stop, so we stop running. How long we walk after that, I don't know. I am just so tired. I don't know if I can walk anymore. My right leg, the one with the shrapnel, hurts too bad. And still this journey with no known destination goes on for what seems like forever. I am again out of strength, and so once again, Sidan carries me most of the way.

After the first few days the food we brought with us is all but gone.

I know this causes Mom and Dad grave concern as they now have seven young mouths to feed. (Sovannara, my baby sister, was born while we were in Battambang.)

Thankfully, at least for now, there are a few alternatives to starving. The villagers who live in the countryside come out of their homes and huts and watch as we pass.

They have rice, which we need. And being from the city, some of us have money, gold, and nice clothes… which they want. So many of the families, including mine, begin trading our belongings with the farmers in exchange for food.

Often there are fruit trees lining the side of the road that offer something edible. However, you cannot just pick the fruit as the tree may be on someone's property. You must ask permission first. Sometimes they let you have it and sometimes they don't. Even in such times, the hearts of some are stone.

At some point in the journey we get to stop and rest. This respite lasts for a few days… maybe even as long as a week. People sleep in cars or trucks or on blankets they brought along. Some put up simple makeshift tents of straw and bamboo using saws, hoes, axes, and other tools they borrow from the villagers. Some of the villagers even pitch in to help. I don't know if the soldiers ask them to help or they just do it out of their own good heart.

This bit of rest is appreciated, of course. But it is here, while we are stopped, that the war takes its first casualty on our family.

My younger sister, and baby of the family, Sovannara (not to be confused with my older sister, Sovannary), is not yet three years old. Within the first two days of this pause in our travels our family's little baby girl dies of malnutrition.

My mom and dad have to bury her there in that place, that awful place. Sidan, my oldest brother by eight years, helps dig her grave. Mercifully, I am not allowed to watch.

I guess in retrospect the only grace I can see in this is that at least we were already stopped for a few days, allowing time to bury her. Had we been moving, I'm not sure what would have happened to her. We are quickly learning to be thankful for small mercies.

Our journey to the countryside takes about three weeks. But to me it seems like an eternity. We end up in Moung Ruessei, 83 kilometers (51.5 miles) south of Battambang, the place we will now call home – one family member short.

So many people died on this nightmarish and cruel *journey*. A lot more are close to death now. And still many, many more will die in the days to come. Remember, we have been on a forced *hike* for nearly a month now.

Moung Ruessei offers makeshift straw huts crowded together in rows like one big campground. Thousands of families need shelter, and although the rows of straw huts stretch as far as you can see, there are not enough huts for everyone.

This means many of the families, including ours, have to build their own hut. The Khmer Rouge supply bamboo, straw, and tools that they confiscate from the villagers. Dad and Mom, along with my oldest brother and sister, put up our hut. A fellow traveler helps them.

I like to think of where we live now as a neighborhood – or maybe even a village or community. But it does not matter what I call it. What matters is what the Khmer Rouge call it, because that is the most accurate description of what it truly is. And they call it a *workcamp*, for reasons you will soon understand.

3

The Difference a Year Makes

Our new family home in Moung Ruessei is little more than a dirt-floor straw hut in one of the endless rows of similar straw huts in the workcamp. At the same time, what's ironic is that the workcamp is set in one of the many beautiful, bright green lush landscapes of jungle and rice paddies abounding throughout Cambodia.

The camp, fully populated with those who were forced to leave the city, is divided into groups. There are about 50 families per group. There are around 10 groups in our camp, which gives you some idea of the size of the camp.

The Khmer Rouge use the first month we are there to get everyone accustomed to what life in the workcamp will be like. Though no one has to work that first month, there are other things to learn. And we are still required to get up at a certain time every morning. The soldiers either wake you using the loudspeakers or by going up and down the rows of huts yelling orders.

One thing families learn that first month is how to forage – which means the adults and children that are old enough and healthy enough have to get out and search for food. Keep in mind, these are city people, not exactly experts at jungle survival.

But it soon becomes clear that whether you make it or not is of no concern to the Khmer Rouge. In terms of food, all they provide is a small, once-a-day ration of watery rice porridge. That's it. The adults have no choice, then, but to learn how to find what food they can in the wild for themselves and their children.

Imagine that many people crammed into one place. And all must scour the fields and waterways for whatever edibles they can find to stay alive.

In the shallow water you might catch shrimp, crabs, or snails. In deeper waters you can sometimes find fish. And, of course, anything that moves on the ground, even down to rodents, grubs, and insects, is considered food.

At the edge of the jungle near and around the rice fields you might also luck up on some edible plants. One that is especially good to eat is called *morning glory* (different from the American plant with the same name), and another called *tracoun*, both similar to spinach.

It would be hard enough for a small village of families to survive on what they can forage from their surroundings. Imagine the challenge when your family is one of *500 families* trying to find enough to keep their little ones alive and themselves strong enough to work. It is nerve racking. I know Mom and Dad worry themselves sick over it.

The soldiers regularly shout demands over the loudspeakers. They order people to get their huts built. They bark commands telling us when and where to go for food rations, when to get up and when to go to bed, and all the other tasks that are required of us.

Every order, every sound, that comes through those loudspeakers rattles my bones. It is terrifying, especially to someone my age. Though I am never far from Dad or Mom or my older brothers and sisters, every time I hear that sound, I run to one of them. At first, it scares me and my two closest brothers (in age) so bad that our parents and older siblings instinctively grab us and hold us until it stops. After a couple of weeks, we all just get numb to it.

The first month we are here the soldiers busily group everybody into categories by "working order." In other words, they separate those they decide are able to work from those who are not. Some are exempt; small children and the elderly do not work, for example. Everyone else either works… or they are killed. If they decide you are able to work and for whatever reason you do not… or cannot… you are shot on the spot.

And if you do not work *hard* enough to suit them, they put a bag over your head and suffocate you and then throw your body into the field to rot. In their eyes, you are not even worth wasting a bullet on.

Though able-bodied workers are essential to their mission, to the Khmer Rouge you as an individual are *completely disposable.* It is obvious they are not concerned at all with keeping workers well and strong so they can continue working. To the contrary – they could care less if you starve to death.

Each group of families is appointed a leader to oversee that group, and then the camp as a whole has an overseer. Each group leader is responsible to report misconduct inside their group to the camp overseer.

The Khmer Rouge also use spies, particularly at night. These are often kids and others living in the workcamp who are charged with scoping out and reporting anything out of line. These spies, called "chlop" (pronounced "tchloe"), are ordered to report anyone trying to escape or steal food to the overseer.

Thankfully, not all the group leaders are bad. Sometimes they look the other way. Even so, that is no comfort, because you never know whether they will or won't. There is an added insidiousness to this. It turns the helpless against one another.

Workers report to the group leader every morning in order to get their assignments. Of course, every person must be accounted for. And if you do anything out of line – like staying gone too long to relieve yourself or get caught eating something that is off limits – you are definitely threatened, likely beaten, or possibly killed.

Sometimes even children are yelled at and beaten. (I never heard of a child being killed, but that does not mean it didn't happen.)

Those who have been sorted out as workers begin working in the rice fields under the guard's watchful eye – from dawn to dusk, seven days a week. That includes both Dad and Mom, of course. My oldest sister Sovannary (she is 12 years older than me) is assigned to light work to begin with. But as soon as she turns 16, she must keep the same schedule as the adults. (For boys, it is even worse. Boys have to leave the family at 14.)

Rain or shine, it makes no difference; everyone of age works in the rice fields. They plow, plant, pick, bag, and replant… anything and everything that is required to grow, produce, and harvest the rice for market has to be done by these "workers."

You would think if you are working in the rice fields you could surely have rice to eat. That would be logical. But that is not at all how it works. Every bit of rice the workers produce is sold as a commodity, mostly to China. If you are found taking any of the rice outside your daily rationed amount, you are beaten or shot.

Just a few months earlier these same workers lived in comfortable homes in the city. They had respectable jobs for which they earned a decent wage. Their children went to school. Their wives chatted with friends as they shopped for food in the town's markets.

And now they are slaves to the Khmer Rouge, forced to work the rice fields in the sweltering heat on very little sleep and almost no food. They are held hostage to a maniacal and tyrannical regime, with little hope and with no end in sight.

Most every night someone is singled out, taken from their family and from the camp, by Khmer Rouge soldiers. They disappear into the night, never to be seen again by anyone.

Every night your family is spared is a good night, though you know your time will come sooner or later. And when it does, you work doubly hard to keep yourself from imagining what happened to your loved one once they are taken. Otherwise you will go mad with worry and grief.

Those they single out are always the intellectuals. They ask people who know you about your history, and they do their own searching into the historical information available to them in the cities and towns.

Sometimes, as I noted earlier, they just make assumptions based on the color of your skin, or the fact that you wear glasses, or because they already have you marked as someone who worked for the government. As horrific as it sounds, you could be shot if the soldiers at hand merely suspect or *feel like* you aren't aligned with their cause!

You may be wondering why they go to all that trouble to empty the cities, march all of us way out to the countryside, just to either kill us or let us die. They have their reasons – revenge, control, a supposed utopia – or just the mad intoxication of power. None of their horrendous acts or devious intents can be justified, of course. But that never seems to matter.

The only reason they keep us around at all is because they want to get all the production out of us that they can before we die of exhaustion, disease, or starvation… or from being killed by them more directly.

As you already know, during the journey from Battambang to Moung Ruessei our original family of nine – Mom, Dad, and seven children – was cut to eight. We lost the youngest member of our family, my sister Sovannara, to starvation before we even got to the workcamp.

I'm sure you can imagine how difficult it is to talk about your family's personal losses and pain. This explains why, for the most part, I am simply recounting these experiences and sharing the facts. As a young child of four or five, I feel terror, loss, sadness. But there is no way I can put my feelings into words. I can only feel what is happening. And it feels so awful. Worse than awful.

Within a few months after arriving at the workcamp we all get sick from malnutrition. Sidan, my oldest brother, is nothing but skin and bone. Sovannary, my oldest sister, has to help him do most everything because he is so weak… including when he has to go to the *hole* beyond the edge of the jungle that we use for a toilet.

This is the point in the story where I am given a nickname. The people in the camp start calling me *Haem* (Khmer for "swollen"), because of my distended abdomen… a gift from starvation.

The possibility, no, the reality of starvation begins taking its toll on others in my family. Within only a handful of months after arriving at the workcamp, the darkest of possibilities strikes our family again. We lose another loved one to starvation. Sotheavy, my next-to-oldest sister, is only 14 years old when she dies.

This regime of tyranny is systematically killing off members of my family one by one. Words cannot convey what is happening to us – and others all around us. It is beyond imaginable. And it is not just a tragic story. It is *real*. It is evil, sickening, hopeless.

Watching little more than the skeletons of two beautiful daughters who were formerly so full of life die in front of you is more than any parent or sibling can manage. These experiences leave the rest of us angry, confused, broken, shattered. The pain is so deep my parents never even speak of it.

But death is nowhere near finished with us. Mom was pregnant with her last child before we were forced to leave Battambang. So a few months after arriving in Moung Ruessei, another baby is born – this time a boy.

This pitifully frail newborn only lives a few days… not even long enough to get a name. To honor him however, I have given him the name Phoenix Ruessei Ung. My baby brother Phoenix is now the third casualty from our family.

Ever so shortly thereafter, the next one of us to die is Ratanavuth. He is my older brother by six years. Just like the others, he also starves to death.

One day, not long after the tragic loss of Ratanavuth, my next oldest brother, Maliane, and I are sitting on the dirt floor of our hut playing a game called *picking sticks*. (Picking sticks is a game where the players arrange a set of small sticks on the ground and then throw a ball in the air. The object of the game is to pick up a stick before the ball hits the ground. The winner is the one with the most sticks when all the sticks are gone.)

Maliane and I are sitting, playing this game together. He is about eight or nine at the time. And while we are playing, he just slumps over. He complains of being tired and wanting to go lie down.

So I get up and go outside to do something else. The next thing I know my parents are burying him. They make me go inside so I can't watch.

It has been less than a year, and within that time this cruel and vicious Khmer Rouge, this *death dealer*, has taken five of my brothers and sisters. Rest in peace:

Sovannara

Sotheavy

Phoenix Ruessei

Ratanavuth

Maliane

All that is left of us is my dad, my mom, my older sister Sovannary, my older brother Sidan, and me. A full half of my family are now gone.

But death from starvation is not the only method the *Khmer Rouge* use to destroy families. Once a girl turns 16, she is separated from the rest of the family and forced to live with other teenage girls in a separate section of the workcamp. (As noted earlier, for boys, the age is 14.) They must work in the rice fields too, just as hard as the adult workers, but they are kept separate from their families. The cruelty is endless.

Following this dictate, Sovannary is removed from the family. She has just turned 16. In some ways this separation may have been harder on my parents than the five children they have now buried. At least Mom and Dad know that those who died can never be subjected to more suffering.

They don't know what Sovannary is having to endure. She is quite possibly being subjected to potential cruelties that my parents have no way of protecting her from. This must have truly ripped their hearts out.

During that whole forced exodus from the city to the country, some of those from Battambang manage to travel together and stay near each other. They are lucky, at least in that respect. We aren't so lucky. Everyone we meet is a stranger.

Nevertheless, our family makes new friends in the workcamp quickly. However, every encounter, neighborly or otherwise, must be discreet. The group leaders and the spies are always watching.

After a few months of being away, Sovannary is granted permission to visit us. We are all thrilled to have her back, if only for a day. To celebrate, Dad and Sidan go foraging in the rice field to see what they can catch. They set some traps and are rewarded with a few field mice.

When they get home with their fresh catch, Sovannary cleans and prepares the mice for our celebration dinner. In a workcamp, you'd be surprised what passes as a simple pleasure – or as a real treat.

Beyond the obvious reasons, there is another reason why this memory is so precious to me. It is, you see, the only personal memory I have of my father.

I am about four years old the day what family we have left celebrates Sovannary's homecoming. Mom and Dad host a *party* – such as it is, in our straw hut in the workcamp. The neighbors are invited to celebrate with us and share in our simple feast. Everyone we know is invited to come and enjoy what little we have to enjoy.

It is the best day we have had together since leaving our home in Battambang. Everyone laughs, talks, eats, and shares in our happiness until late evening. As the sun is quietly setting in the west, the insects in the fields start to sing. You can smell the night air and the scent of onion grass as the breeze floats softly by.

Of course, the pleasantness is tainted with the faint smell of rotting corpses somewhere. But that odor is our constant companion. Although you never get used to it, at least this evening no one seems to notice.

As our cooking fire burns lower and lower, suddenly two uninvited guests – soldiers – step out of the darkness. At their arrival, a collective gasp and even a near scream (from Sovannary) erupts from our little group. This is followed by a heavy, collective, dread-filled silence.

The two soldiers, wearing those all-too-familiar red-checkered scarves, black pants, black tops, and green military caps also have guns, of course. (I will later learn that these rifles are the fierce AK47.)

They stand there – a menacing evil towering over our little group of family and friends. They call out my dad's name in a gruff, threatening tone… *"NEAK UNG!"*

Dad looks at them in response.

"Come with us!"

Dad is visibly shaken. Startled. He hesitates, but only for a few seconds. He has been expecting this. We all have. Still, even knowing it is inevitable, it's the kind of thing you can never prepare for.

Dad knows exactly what is happening. He knows all too well that this will be the last time he sees his dear wife and children. Everyone else knows it too.

"Come with us… or the whole family will be killed!"

Dad takes a few steps forward. They turn him around and tie his hands behind his back. Then they take him away.

I cannot describe the horror I feel, watching my dad walk away between those two soldiers, disappearing into the pitch-black night. It is as if the space around us has become a vacuum. There is no air left to breathe. Everyone is in shock.

I am afraid to move… afraid to look at Mom or my brother or sister. No one dare say what they feel, or worse – what they imagine is about to happen to our *Rock* – our beloved dad. No one breathes even a word of empathy or grief that Dad, the strength of our family, has just been forced into the darkness of a cruel, painful death… alone.

Because we know it will do no good.

It is obvious that Sovannary wants to hold onto him so he can't go. But she knows if she does, they will take her too. She just stands there bawling, helpless as a stone, completely inconsolable, as she watches our father being taken senselessly away. This is the heavy burden Sovannary carries back with her when she returns, all alone, to her group the next day.

Though your head tells you otherwise, your heart cannot bear accepting the fact that your father will never return. Or that he is dead. You have to go on, and to go on you need some sliver of hope to hold onto.

So you keep telling yourself that you just saw him being taken away. Maybe the soldiers took him to another workcamp. Maybe one day he will be allowed to return to his family. Maybe….

All I know for sure is that this life-sucking Khmer Rouge continue to slowly, methodically, unmercifully kill our family little by little. Piece by piece. Member by member.

There were ten Ungs before. Now, in our simple dirt-floored straw hut, all that remains together of my biological family is Mom, Sidan, and me. Just three gutted souls trying our best to survive for the sake of each other. We try to take what comfort we can from the fact that Sovannary is still alive. Still out there… somewhere.

4

Trouble at Tonle Sap

Words can never describe the degree of pain and loss Mom suffered during those first two years after we were forced to leave Battambang. Between 1975 and 1977, she watched five of her children die of starvation while under her care, completely unable to prevent it. She stood helpless while her only remaining daughter, barely a teenager, was forced to leave home and the presence of her family for another workcamp.

The rest of what little strength Mom has left completely drains from her soul as she stands motionless while armed soldiers steal her husband away. The last few vestiges of this fragile family are now in pieces at her feet.

And yet she must find some way to go on, for she still has three children. And even then, there are only two of us she can still *mother* – my older brother, Sidan, and me. As you know, Sovannary has been taken away from us.

Mom is still reeling from that last blow when the Khmer Rouge decide we have to move again. They need workers to go deeper into the countryside to clear brush for planting more rice.

So Mom, Sidan, and I are forced from the workcamp we had come to know as home. We are herded off to some new place to help clear the dense, jungle brush and set up another workcamp.

Needless to say, this move is even more absurd than the forced move to

27

Moung Ruessei. By this point, Mom is terribly broken and so very weak. She is certainly not strong enough to uproot again, let alone to begin clearing brush and building a new *"home."*

Sidan is 13 at the time, still too young to do much on his own. And I am five. But none of this matters, of course. We have no choice. In the eyes of the Khmer Rouge, we, the dispossessed, are not even *people*.

This new place is called Tonle Sap because its land borders the Tonle Sap lake and river. (*Tonle* means "river" in the Khmer language, and *Sap* means "fresh.") So this region gets its name from the freshwater lake that defines it. It is not surprising to hear that fish are plentiful here as a result. But that's it… in terms of food.

A new calamity hits the camp at Tonle Sap. For some unknown reason, a good many of those who are forced to move with us soon contract malaria.

Mom gets real sick too, not long after we get here. I don't know if it's malaria, but she is terribly sick. Perhaps she is just sick from the toll of her suffering. Maybe she has just reached her limit.

But whatever the illness, she is carried to the hospital in Moung Ruessei (horrifyingly, it is run by the Khmer Rouge). She is taken there on a wooden wagon that workers from the jungle use as a hauling cart to bring supplies into the camp.

This leaves Sidan and me alone… at the workcamp in the jungle at Tonle Sap. Sidan is required to work in the fields, of course. So I do too.

Rice is planted in the rainy season. The first step in rice planting is to clean the fields of all the grass, and the rainwater helps loosen the soil. This makes it easier to plow. Once plowed, the soil becomes muddy and the roots of the grass loosen.

During the rainy season my job is to pull and collect the loose grass from the field. I work in the muddy field all day long so, of course, I stay covered in mud. The only recognizable features are my big round eyes and matted, upward-sticking hair. During the harvest, my job is to pick up rice that has been dropped on the ground during the harvest and put it in a pile so it will not be wasted.

With both parents now gone, Sidan becomes a father figure to me.

And considering his age and the circumstances, he is incredibly good at taking care of us. He has become quite skilled at hunting and gathering. So thankfully we do not go hungry nearly as often now.

But even this little victory is bittersweet. The only reason Sidan and I have more to eat is because we have so much less family now.

He is all I have left in the world, so naturally I don't want him out of my sight. Wherever he goes, I tag along. Whatever he does, I stay right with him, making sure I don't lose him too.

My need to stay close is problematic, however, when he has to gather food for us. I am too small to be of help in this, and it is faster and safer and more efficient if he forages and hunts alone.

So when he needs to go looking for food, he tries getting me busy doing something so he can sneak out. Of course, as soon as I realize he is gone I cry. And since we have to eat every day, this happens daily. Once he tricked me into going to sleep, but I woke up and caught him sneaking out. I screamed so loud that he had to come back.

Sometimes he hunts during the day and sometimes at night. We eat whatever he can find. We're not picky.

Fish is the highlight of our menu. We also eat a lot of field mice (rats) and eels. The secret to catching rats is to smoke them out using burning leaves from the coconut trees.

Sidan is truly amazing; he always finds a way to get us just enough food to keep us from starving. Some days he is successful on his hunting/gathering expeditions and other days he is not. But on those days when we have nothing new to eat, we eat the leftovers he rationed from a day we had plenty. Had it not been for him there is no way I could have survived. Can you see why he is a hero to me?

Sidan is not only good at hunting for food, he is also skilled at stealing rice from the rice factory. None of us has any reservations whatsoever about doing this, when we can get away with it. These are desperate times, and everyone does what they have to do to survive. And after all, it is our oppressors that we are stealing from.

When rice is harvested, it is cut at the stem and taken to the makeshift factory where the kernels are removed from the stem. The next step in the process removes the husk, leaving the brown rice. Brown rice goes through yet another stage of processing where the brown coating is removed, leaving only the white kernel that is then milled and freed of impurities.

Thanks to the slave labor of the workers, tons and tons of rice are produced, processed, canned, and sold to other countries for a profit by the Khmer Rouge. It's ironic that all the while the workers themselves are dying of starvation.

At some point I decide I need to help my brother. I'm only five, and not near so savvy as Sidan. But he is stealing rice from the factory… everybody we know is stealing rice from the factory… why can't I do it too?

So one day I sneak off by myself and somehow manage to pilfer one can of rice. Thinking I have accomplished something amazing, I run as fast as I can out of the building. But before I hardly clear the door, a blind man standing on guard for looters like me catches me right outside the entrance. He reaches out and happens to grab my arm and stop me. He asks if I have stolen any rice, and I say "yes."

"Well, you better give me that rice you stole, or else I'll tell them at the factory what you've done."

So I reluctantly hand over the can of rice that I had just so proudly stolen.

When I get home and tell Sidan about it, he first gets mad at me… and then at the blind man. He storms out of our shanty and chases the blind man down and takes the rice back!

To this day I cannot steal, cheat, or lie. I'm certainly no angel and never expect to be. But the blind man working outside a rice plant for the Khmer Rouge that day *scared me to death.*

Even with our father now dead, and our mother away in a hospital, it seems to my young mind, in some strange way, that life is normal enough because I still have Sidan. I do not understand why everyone is gone or where they went. All I know is that Sidan is still here.

Of course, I want Mom and Dad to come back home. I want the rest of my family to be here too. But they are not. Sidan is. And somehow my young heart and mind are able to content themselves with that.

Then one day tragedy visits us again. While looking for food, Sidan falls out of a coconut tree he climbed to get us some coconuts. He breaks both of his legs. I am not there to see it, as I am working in a nearby field.

One of the overseers of our workcamp finds out and runs to tell Sovannary (in a nearby workcamp) what happened. Thankfully, whoever is in charge that day is kind enough to let her go to him.

When she finds him, he is lying on the ground with the femurs of both legs jabbing through the skin. Compound fractures.

Not only that, but either as a result of the fall or the strain from being in so much pain, one of his eyes has popped out of its socket.

And he is not moving at all. Sovannary thinks he is dead.

But as Providence would have it, one of those same rickety wagons drawn by cattle that took Mom to the hospital happens by. Some people help lift Sidan onto the wagon so they can take him to the hospital where Mom is. And Sovannary goes with him. Because of the urgency of the situation, there is no time to wait for someone to fetch me, so she has to leave me behind.

Again, thanks to Providence, while they are on their way to the hospital at Moung Ruessei (the one controlled by the Khmer Rouge), they pass a military truck with a dark green cabin and canvas tarp over the back.

Sovannary asks the driver (referred to as a *courier*) of the truck if he can take Sidan to the hospital. She is afraid he will bleed to death before they can get there in the wagon. The courier agrees, but he tells them they should go to the military hospital instead of the hospital in Moung Ruessei. So they move Sidan into the back of the truck and head to the military hospital.

As soon as they get there, the doctor suggests they amputate both of his legs. But my sister refuses, and instead demands a second opinion. Because she is so adamant on this matter, she gets her way.

The second doctor recommends some strange, old-school way of putting Sidan's legs back together instead of cutting them off. She pleads with him to do that rather than amputating. Thankfully, he consents.

It takes three months for Sidan's legs to heal, so he and Sovannary stay at the military hospital for the duration. For these same three months Mom is still in the Moung Ruessei hospital.

And I am all alone… a five-year-old, alone in a communist workcamp.

To be honest, my memory of those months I spent alone is very fragmented. They are like scenes in a dream; they come in bits and pieces and I don't remember what came first or next in sequence.

But as it turns out, a neighbor lady who lived in the nearby countryside must have taken pity on me, because she tries to take me in. I say *tries,* because I do not like going to her house for some reason. Maybe it's just one adjustment too many for my young mind.

She comes to get me in the evening to eat and sleep, but sometimes I wake up in the middle of the night and walk back to my hut and sleep by myself. If I stay at her house, I usually sleep in the corner of a room with some chickens she has.

The next morning, I am covered in chicken poop! It doesn't bother me that much, though. Most kids have a high tolerance for getting dirty; I guess mine is higher than most. Or perhaps it is just that, in a reality as horrifying as mine is, what's a little chicken poop.

In addition to working in the rice fields during the day when I am more-or-less on my own, I remember doing chores for this lady and other adults who live around her. Some of those chores include collecting dried coconut leaves, wood, and straw that they use for fires. Burning coconut leaves creates a lot of smoke, which helps when collecting honey from beehives and flushing out mice from their holes for meat.

My other jobs include collecting cow and pig dung (used for fertilizer) and feeding livestock. I also use a hoe to break up the ground for sowing. There is a good reason why I remember using that hoe. One day I split my big toe open with it!

Three months after the accident, Sidan and Sovannary finally return home together. Sidan's legs are healing, but ever so slowly. He still cannot walk; but at least he is finally well enough to leave the hospital.

When they get home, they find me sleeping on a filthy mat covered in, you guessed it, *chicken poop.* Sovannary says I look as if I had not been bathed the whole time she was gone, which is probably true. Her response when she saw me, in the Khmer language, was: "He is filthy, dirty, and stinky with the look of malnourishment."

She grabs a bucket of water and scrubs me from head to toe, trying to remove the multiple layers of dirt that have dried into my skin. But water is not strong enough to make any difference. She borrows kerosene from the neighbor to bathe me in, just to remove all the dried-in dirt!

All three of us are now home, but since Sidan still cannot walk, Sovannary and I are responsible for finding our food. Sidan has not lost his fighting spirit, however. His injury and lack of mobility actually makes him mad, so he starts getting around by "walking" on his butt across the dirt floor. He forces himself to exercise his legs – do his own version of physical therapy, you might say – and as a result is able to walk again within a few weeks of coming home.

There is a sad side to Sidan's recovery, however. Once he is well enough, Sovannary has to leave us again to return to her workcamp.

Within a few months, miraculously Sidan's legs heal completely and he is back to hunting, gathering, and stealing rice again. It must have been a good season, because before long we have plenty to eat. In fact, we have so many leftovers that we decide to take some to Mom in the hospital.

When I think about it now, I can't believe Mom was sick that long. She has been gone for about nine months by now. And since the Khmer Rouge own the hospital – and they know our Dad worked for the government – I wonder whether she is actually sick this whole time.

Maybe instead, it is part of their subversive attack on our family by removing one more member... this time, our mom. Or maybe she is just actually that sick. She certainly has plenty reason to be.

Sidan and I pack enough food for us, and for Mom, and start out. The hospital is a long way off. It's about a day and a half of travel on foot over some very treacherous terrain.

Those long dirt roads seem to never end. Tall trees line the roads, with little else to change the scenery except for an occasional hut. If you walk the roads at night, you must also try to avoid the guerillas – those Khmer Rouge vigilantes who are always on the lookout for deserters. If they see you, they shoot you.

So at the first sign, sound, or sight of them, we quickly duck into the nearby brush and wait. You never know where they are, of course. If you see distant lights on either side of the road, it could be someone's house or hut. Or it could be their camp. You have no way of knowing, so you are never safe… or relaxed.

During the day you can better tell the workers from the guerillas. We sometimes ask villagers if we can stay with them. Most do not let us, for fear of being questioned and maybe killed for taking us in. But a few do let us stay long enough to rest and to maybe share a meal. More often than not, however, we have to work for even a bowl of rice.

Unfortunately, I get tired walking after a while. So Sidan, just 13 himself – and after recovering from two broken legs – carries me on his back. It is muddy, making the trek even harder.

I complain of being hungry and often cry. Sidan is just as malnourished as I am. But somehow he does what he has to do because he is determined for us both to get to see Mom.

After what seems like forever, we finally make it to the hospital. I stay in some kind of waiting room while Sidan goes in to find our mother. Inside are rows and rows of beds packed together, almost on top of each other. And it seems no one is caring for these people.

Knowing what I know now, there is probably a shortage of medically trained staff. By all evidence, the workers here probably couldn't care less whether you live or die. Their mission has never been to keep us alive.

Sidan looks all over and cannot find Mom. So he starts asking around. Eventually, one of the patients points to an empty bed. The only thing on the bed is a backpack that Sidan recognizes.

"Where's my mom?"

"She's gone," the patient responds. "She passed a few days ago."

Sidan continues asking until someone tells him that her body was buried somewhere behind the hospital. Of course, we can find out nothing about what was wrong with her or how she died.

In addition to whatever illness she had, I can only imagine how she was treated. Our family was tagged as enemies of the regime, and the Khmer Rouge's reputation speaks for itself.

As soon as he realizes she is actually gone, Sidan breaks down and cries. And when he tells me, I do too.

It feels like the ground has just opened up beneath us. We believed all this time that Mom was still alive and would one day come back home.

And when she didn't, as soon as Sidan was well enough and we had food enough to share with her, we determined we would come to her.

But now she's gone. Who knows? Maybe if we had come just a few days earlier at least we could have seen her before she died. There is nothing left now to hope for… but that she was buried with some dignity. At least that would be something.

The pain is overwhelming. The Ung body count is now two sisters, four brothers, our dad, and now our mom. Suddenly, this all is more than a couple of young boys can bear.

All that's left of our once large family is our sister Sovannary, Sidan, and me. And Sovannary cannot even be with us, which means that it's just Sidan – a scrawny, malnourished 13-year-old, and me – a confused, exhausted, hungry, scared, brokenhearted, bony-yet-swollen five-year-old.

How in the world do we make it on our own? And how can we keep going when every last piece of our world is systematically being snatched from us?

5

False Hope

We have no clue what to do or where to go, other than to try and get to our sister. Somehow, Sidan remembers where she is. I guess his survival mechanism kicks in yet again, and he figures it out. So we leave the hospital and head in her direction.

We are now faced with more days of walking barefoot over these rocky roads… begging what food we can along the way. At the same time, we know we must stay vigilant or we'll be the next ones to go.

We are scared, for sure. But we are just too sad to be scared enough… and too tired to be sad enough. Just trying to survive, most of our strength goes to keeping our eyes and ears peeled. We can feel our fear with every step of that long, grueling journey.

We finally get to the rice field where Sovannary is working with other young women in her camp. Somebody calls out her name when they realize we are looking for her. When she looks up, she sees Sidan. And sadly, she sees that he is carrying the backpack with Mom's belongings.

"Mom is dead." Instinctively, Sovannary's mind and heart tell her this before we ever get to her.

Sidan starts running toward her. They hold each other for such a long time, sobbing there in the middle of the field. Sovannary cries so hard that everybody around them stops working. They all understand. They have all lost family too; they know what she is feeling. Our suffering is as communal as it is personal.

While standing there hopeless and broken, in the middle of that rice field, Sovannary starts yelling out the names of every one of our family members who has either died or been killed. On seeing all this, the head of the work group gives her permission to grieve with her brothers... *for an hour.*

We cannot stay at the women's camp; it is against the rules. But at least for a little while the three of us are all together and that feels good.

When Sidan and I have to leave, we head back to the original work-camp in Moung Ruessei where our family had initially been forced to move to. No one tells us to, but it doesn't make sense to go back to the jungle when our mother is no longer working there. Besides, it is farther away. Why put ourselves through further danger.

Then one day Sovannary gets permission to come visit us at Moung Ruessei. She tells us about a different workcamp that she is being transferred to. She also tells us about a lady who lives not far from there who is too old to work for herself. She has already talked to the woman, who wants us to stay with her and help her. And in exchange for doing her chores she will feed and house us.

We don't ask permission from the leaders of our workcamp for the simple fact that they wouldn't have given it. But we know the Khmer Rouge can't watch everybody every minute, so we decide to risk it.

I think too, after all we've been through, *we just don't care anymore.* Sometimes you just have nothing more to give.

So one night, deep into that night, we escape from our camp and are able to find our way to the woman's hut. It's hard to put into words just how risky this action is, for had we been caught we would have been shot.

This lady certainly has a lot more food than we are used to. We fairly gorge ourselves on fruit and whatever else she offers us. We stay with her and help her for as long as we can get away with it.

(You have no doubt noted how often I refer to our scouring and pleading for food, and you will read still more of that in the pages to come. I cannot express the anxiety that comes with merely trying to get enough to eat just to stay alive. It gives you a full appreciation for the well-known prayer, *"Give us this day our daily bread."*)

One day, all too soon, two soldiers come to the lady's hut and tell her Sidan and I must leave. Sidan has to go live in the teenage boy's camp now, because he is 14. And I am taken to live with a group of younger boys... somewhere.

I always get this sick feeling in the pit of my stomach when I see soldiers. I know they are not there to share good news. In my gut I figured something like this would eventually happen. But Sidan tells me to listen to them, do what they say, and not to worry. And by now I know we have no choice, want to or not.

What really terrifies me now is that not even Sidan, my mainstay, knows where I am. But to keep from falling apart, I lie to myself and say that he *does* know.

In reality though, I am alone. Once again.

It is now 1978. The Khmer Rouge have been in power for three years and our beautiful country is ravaged. And though some version of this crazy civil war is still going on, all the people in *our* world are just trying to beat disease, famine, exhaustion... and of course, starvation. At least there is no fighting around us. And I am grateful for that.

But then something happens that changes the direction of everything. It opens the door to a whole new chapter in our lives. And it comes in the middle of the night – in the form of a train.

The Khmer Rouge have joined forces with the North Vietnamese to fight the Cambodian resistance. And though none of us prisoners of the workcamps has any way of knowing what is happening with the war itself, there is a story going around that we eventually hear.

The North Vietnamese use trains to move weapons and supplies from their country to the Khmer Rouge in Cambodia. As the story goes, one night while transporting a load of weapons, one of their trains explodes. For some reason (perhaps *hope against hope*) it becomes a shared belief that this signifies the last stand of the North Vietnamese and the Khmer Rouge against the resistance.

This means, so the belief goes, that the Khmer Rouge are no longer in power… *that we are now free!*

This version of the story is very appealing, of course. You can imagine how news about the overthrow of this maniacal regime is the best word we can hear, and news we've all longed for!

In a quiet moment, I stop to think that the exploding train is a symbol of everything that has happened to us since this senseless war started. Our family, our lives have also been *blown up*. Very little is left of our once beautiful world… the world we were forced in an instant to leave behind. All that is now left of that world is three siblings.

It is amazing how some obscure news about an explosion on a train can reawaken a measure of hope and enthusiasm. Little do we know, however, that we are not yet done with the famine, the sufferings, the killing – the *hard*.

While we are sorting things out as best we can, our aunt (our mom's sister), uncle, and their children – all seven of them – are facing their own set of challenges.

My cousin, Malis, shares a bit of their story:

My father, a physician, is Head of Nursing at the Battambang hospital when the Khmer Rouge take control of our province. Ten other doctors and 20 nurses work with my father at the hospital. Within a couple of months after taking control of Battambang, the Khmer Rouge *track down and kill every single one of them!*

Of course, my father's name is on their *hit list* as well.

Thankfully, a communist soldier whose wife had earlier been treated for an illness by my father risks his life to secretly inform Father that they will be coming for him next.

He tells my father he needs to escape immediately if he wants to have any chance of survival. He also tells him that, in fact, our entire family is on the list to be killed, probably because my mother is also educated. She is a nurse.

He describes how the Khmer Rouge are killing people using a 10-kilo (22-pound) hammer blow to the back of the head. (They do this to save their bullets!) This really worries my father.

If he must be killed, he much prefers to be shot.

I can't put into words for you what it's like to be at the mercy of this kind of malevolent power. Like their victims, the Khmer Rouge are

Cambodian! And yet they treat us like animals and hunt us down as such. So much so that to kill us, they prefer to hit their fellow countrymen in the back of the head with a hammer – as though slaughtering a pig – rather than *waste* a bullet on us.

Malis continues:

That very night Father begins hiding out in a grove of banana trees close to our house. From the tops of the trees he can see when the communist soldiers come looking for him. His plan is to run so they will have to shoot him instead of capturing him. He doesn't want to die via that hammer blow to the head.

On the third night after my father leaves, two soldiers come to the house looking for him. But thankfully, these soldiers are not Khmer Rouge. They are from the opposition communist movement stationed along the Cambodian-Thai border. They desperately need a doctor at their hospital, and someone tells them my father is the only local doctor still alive.

Once we hear their story, Mother explains where he is and what he is planning to do. My sister goes and gets him, and Father leaves with those two soldiers that same night.

The next morning Mother makes up a story to tell the head of the community in hopes that the rest of the family will be spared. She tells him that my father beat her the night before and now he has run away.

They send guards to look for him. Three days later they find a man that fits his description who had hung himself on a tamarind tree. They believe my mother's story, and so our lives are spared.

Nearly four years later, on January 7, 1979, Vietnamese soldiers take control of Cambodia's government and force Pol Pot's communist party out of power. Thankfully, this breaks the back of the Khmer Rouge in terms of being in control of our country as a whole.

But we face another survival problem. Food is frightfully scarce. There are eight of us and as the oldest child, I have the responsibility of finding food to support the family. This is a very difficult time for our family, and many days we have almost nothing to eat between us.

Living in Battambang, we are only about 90 km (56 miles) from the Thai border. People often travel to the border to buy food from the Thai people. My mother decides that if our family is to survive, we must escape to the border in hopes of finding my father… and food.

Even though Pol Pot is no longer in power, there are still pockets of communist Khmer Rouge hidden throughout the jungle areas. They may have lost most of their power, but their commitment is still intact. They are lying in wait with the intent of killing anyone attempting to leave Cambodia.

But that is not our only challenge. In addition, the Thai soldiers are stationed all along the border in order to keep communists from coming into their country.

Escaping Cambodia is risky business as a result, so we must be as careful and discreet as possible. Mother believes that if we split up into two groups and leave at different times, we have the best chance of making it to the border.

So, my mother and four of my siblings leave first. Two weeks later my two younger siblings and I escape with the hopes of rejoining her and the rest of my family at the border.

The area my mother and siblings come to first is a refugee camp called *New Camp*. And one of the first people she meets there is one of my father's friends who is also a doctor. In fact, he's the doctor in charge at the camp, and when he hears about our situation, he offers my mother a job as his assistant. This provides the money we need to buy food.

A couple of weeks later, the remainder of my family (my siblings and I) arrive at the border safely as well. To our great joy and surprise, eventually my father learns that his family is living at New Camp, and he comes to find us. We are so thankful we are all alive and all reunited and able to live as one family again!

6

The Little Wooden House in the Country

The weakening of the Khmer Rouge I mentioned in the last chapter has made a significant difference for those of us in the workcamps. The fact that they are no longer guarding us gives us freedom of movement. As a consequence of that mobility, Sovannary, Sidan, and I are able to reunite. We have no idea what to do, but at least we can now do it together.

Then Sovannary has an idea about where the three of us might go. While working at the teenage girls' camp, she heard of a refugee camp in Thailand that is right on the border. Not only did that sound like the most reasonable option, it is the *only* option she and Sidan can come up with. So as soon as the decision is made, we head out walking in the direction of the border.

Here we are, three kids attempting a journey that will take weeks on foot – or more accurately, on bare feet – over rocky, dirt roads and potentially through pockets of residual enemy territory. We are completely on our own, and all we possess in the world is little more than the clothes on our backs.

Someone is kind enough to point us in the right direction and to tell Sovannary what road to take as our beginning. It is a winding dirt road in the country. We have no clue how far it is to this mysterious place called Thailand, how long it will take, nor how we will survive. And we have no reserves of food or water.

As far as we know, the war has ended. But war or no war, we are still hard-wired to constantly be looking out for the Khmer Rouge, especially at night. Even by day, we are sure to remember to keep a low profile. For all we know, they may still be intentionally hunting members of our family down.

We are so hungry and weak… and afraid for our lives. We are sad for what has happened to us, that we have no more family, no mom and no dad. We are neither old enough nor strong enough to deal with the weight of it all.

Because of our extreme emotional and physical exhaustion, very few words pass between us. For me personally, all I really know is that I don't want to live any more.

I wonder if my brother and sister feel the same way. Staying alive is a lot more trouble than it seems worth. I just want to stop and lie down and go to sleep and never wake up. Death has become synonymous with rest.

After hours of walking, we see a house. So we stop. Sovannary asks if we can spend the night. They say no. Everyone is paranoid. Nobody wants to invite more trouble from the Khmer Rouge. It's understandable, but still it's so discouraging.

So we stop at the next house we see. No luck there either. But we are desperate, so we keep trying. After three or four more requests, someone takes pity on us and allows us to stay. The next day we help with chores, picking fruits and doing little jobs for them. In return for helping them, they let us sleep at their hut for one more night.

And then we move on. After another day of walking, we come upon another hut and try again. Thankfully, they too allow us to stay the night in exchange for helping with chores. And then, again, we move on the next morning.

Another day of walking and we see a house in the distance – a little wooden hut in the country. And though it is on stilts like so many wooden houses in the countryside, for some reason this one feels special to us. I can't explain it, but each of us felt it.

It has its own well out back – a little stone well with a wooden roof.

Beyond the well lies acres and acres of gently sloping rice fields. And bordering the edge of the rice fields is the jungle. Past the hut on the right side a mountain of lush green jungle trees rises high toward the sky.

A very nice man and lady greet us at the door. The lady is short, but strong looking. Typical of rural Cambodian women, she has the look of one who has done a lot of physical work in her life. She has short black hair – the customary Cambodian country hair that touches the top of her shoulders. It is plain and practical. She is wearing a sarong and a T-shirt, again, typical for adult women who live in the country. (A sarong is a sheet of cloth, cut like a towel, that wraps around your waist and ties with a twist.)

Sovannary does the talking for us –

"Hello. Can you please help us? It's just me and my brothers. The rest of our family is dead. We may have some relatives that survived the war – our aunt and uncle and their family – but I'm not sure. If they did, they are at the refugee camp. In a few days I will leave again to go to the camp and try to find them. But if my brothers could stay here…"

The man and his wife smile and welcome us in with open arms to join the rest of their children.

We stay here one night, and then another, and another. Pretty soon a week's worth of nights pass, and we are still at that house. It is the best thing that has happened to us… for literally years now. We begin to feel like we belong here.

Not long after we arrive, a few other kids find their way here too. And they are met with the same warm welcome.

At one point there are ten children in all, at least half of whom are like us – with no other family and nowhere else to go.

Even though the house is little more than a straw hut, it is a bit larger than most wooden huts. Still, it is not made to accommodate this many people! Nevertheless, this loving couple manages to fit everybody in. Everyone is fed. And we all sleep inside the hut, wherever we can find a place.

During the daytime, while the older kids help with chores, the younger kids play games, using whatever we can find around the house. One day we discover a bicycle wheel, so we each get a stick and push the wheel to see who can push it the farthest. (To this day, I'm unusually fond of bicycle wheels, I don't mind telling you.)

We also play hide-and-seek, freeze tag, stick golf, and a version of hacky sack. (You may know that the hacky sack craze started in Asia. Initially it was a feather attached to a light piece of plastic, kind of like the *birdie* in badminton.)

We have great fun at this little house. In fact, it is the most fun I have ever had as a kid. And somehow there is enough food to feed us all, especially fruits that we pick. In fact, quite often we even have leftovers.

So in spite of the fact that Sovannary, Sidan, and I have lost everything and everyone from our nuclear family – our mom and dad and the rest of our brothers and sisters, as well as our home and all our belongings – this begins to feel like a normal life for the typical family that lives in the country.

In fact, so much do we now feel like a family – my second family – that we take to calling our new "foster" mom and dad, *Mère* and *Père*. (Once again here are words that show the French influence on our language. These terms are French synonyms for Mother and Father.)

After about a month, Sovannary thanks Père and Mère profusely for their kindness and tells them she is leaving for the Thai border to try and find our aunt and uncle and their family. She also tells Sidan, but I'm out playing when she leaves.

As soon as I realize she's gone, I ask Mère, "Where's Sovannary?"

"She left for the refugee camp, hoping to find your aunt and uncle."

I start to cry. Sidan comforts me, of course, telling me it is for the best and that everything will be alright. "Don't worry. We'll see her again soon."

At least I still have Sidan. And he has me. And we have our new foster family.

I am now going to let Sovannary tell you, in her own words, why she chose to set out for the border alone, leaving Sidan and me with Mère and Père and the other orphans. She says:

> My brothers and I are safe enough here with our foster family,
> but it is clear to those of us who are older that food is getting more
> and more scarce. The destruction that comes with war and with
> an evil regime being in power has left our country in a state of

poverty and famine. And if something doesn't change soon, we will all starve to death.

I know of only one option. I hear there is food in Thailand, and that people escape to the border all the time in order to survive starvation. Being the oldest of my siblings, I feel it is my responsibility to see what I can do. So I ask around, and in the process I meet three guides who, for a fee, help people escape to the border.

It is obvious that one of the guides likes me. In fact, I find out later that he likes me so well that he asks around to see what he can find out about my family and my background.

He must be pleased with what he discovers, because he then asks me if I would be willing to marry his nephew who is now at the camp on the Cambodian side of the border.

I seize this as an opportunity to make a deal with him. "If you help me get to the border safely and find my aunt and uncle, then yes, in exchange for your help, I will marry your nephew."

The guide believes he knows my aunt and where she is. That is enough for me. Because our situation is so desperate, I see this as the one opportunity I have to save my brothers and myself. So as hard as it is to say goodbye to Sidan and Sideth, I leave them behind with our foster family with the hope that I can find the rest of our family and then figure out how to come back for them.

I leave with the guide right away, along with a group of 30-40 others wanting to also escape to the border. The advantage to traveling in a group is safety. Everyone is in the same situation. Circumstances have made us a family. We look out for each other. Aside from the danger of the communist Vietnamese or the random pockets of Khmer Rouge still terrorizing those of us trying to escape, I feel safe with this group. Besides, the guides are knowledgeable about when to travel, what places we should avoid, and where to hide when necessary.

After a few days we arrive safely at the border. I go immediately to the hospital there because I know that's where my aunt will be working. Thankfully I find her! She is, of course, as happy to see me as I am her. And what a joy it is to be with my aunt and uncle and cousins again!

That evening around dinner we share what all has happened to us after we were driven from our homes. Through tears and with much grief I explain how all my family – except for Sidan and Sideth and me – were killed or died from starvation.

Aunt Sim is devastated. It is more than she can take in when she learns that her sister and brother-in-law, as well as all her nieces and nephews, except for the three of us, are dead.

Her grief transforms into an agent of her will. From this moment she begins planning how we can bring Sidan and Sideth here to live with us as soon as possible.

I am hardly settled in, however, when war breaks out between the Thai and Cambodian armies stationed along the border. The camp we're at is bombed, and we all have to run for safety. We're so thankful that none of us are hurt… or worse, killed. But we do lose touch with the guide whose nephew I promised to marry. In fact, he may have even been killed himself in the bombing.

After that experience, the United Nations decides to bring most of us living in this current camp – New Camp – to the Khao-I-Dang camp in Thailand where we will be safe. So we all are moved to Khao-I-Dang. That was in early 1980.

A few months later I make the hard decision to leave the comfort of family and return to the refugee camp on the Cambodian side. It is my ongoing belief that I will have a better chance there of connecting with people who may be able to help me get Sidan and Sideth back.

And now you know why my sister, Sovannary – my brave, strong, loving sister – is one of my heroes. To take this journey on would be daunting enough for a grown man. But to face it as a young, beautiful teenage girl (with all the extra risks this brings into play, given there are lawless rebel soldiers possessing the morals of a goat roaming about) is beyond my ability to take in.

A few more months pass. Life is normal once again. Then one day, out of nowhere, a small army of Khmer Rouge soldiers march into our little village in the country. Their telltale "uniform" makes them immediately recognizable. They force everyone in every home in the village to leave. We are herded like cattle to the top of that nearby mountain, the one you can see from our little hut.

Somehow during this day-long exodus from our home, I lose everybody. In the shuffle and confusion of the crowd, I get lost from Sidan, my playmates, Mère and Père… *everybody!*

I am six years old now and once again find myself separated from home and family. Lost in this huge crowd – probably between two and three hundred people – lost and scared to death. I don't know what to do other than just follow the group.

Then out of the corner of my eye, off to the side of the crowd I see this boy sitting on a rock, waving to me. He is one of the kids from the house. He's waiting there just for me! I run toward him.

"Yeah, there you are!" he says. "Come on, we gotta go to Mère! We gotta go over here!"

I take his hand, and we soon find our foster mom. As soon as I get to her, she picks me up. Then she unties the long scarf she has around her neck and wraps it around me, and then reties it around her waist.

I still have no idea what is happening and where we are going, but that's okay now. I am back with my mère. I am literally tied to her! You can't imagine how safe that feels. Then we hurry and find everyone else, including Sidan.

The next thing I know, our whole family is running back down the mountain in an attempt to escape, all the while knowing that the soldiers are armed and can shoot us at any second. (I find out later that they had been looking for me before making their attempted escape – waiting just for me!)

As we run back down the mountain, an airplane flying overhead napalms the whole mountain. (Napalm, if you don't know, is a jelly-like highly flammable petroleum product used in incendiary bombs. It sticks to whatever it hits until it burns out.)

That was the scariest thing I have ever seen in my life. It still gives me chills when I think about it. Of course, I am too young to know what is happening. I just hear this loud boom, then I see a huge fireball, and then a massive cloud of black smoke. I know enough to realize that the mountain has been bombed, and that if our family had not escaped, we would have all been killed in an instant.

Nobody saw it coming. We are just running down the hill to get away from the armed soldiers, and then it all happens. The mountain we have just gotten off of is now engulfed in flames.

Somehow, we all get back down the mountain without injury and start the long hike back to our hut. The journey is at least a day long. On the way we eat whatever fruits and edible plants we can find along the road.

It takes us all a few days to get resettled after that traumatic incident. But then we are soon back to life around the house, playing outside during the day, picking fruits, enjoying that strangely normal life in the country in spite of everything. And thankfully, all of us who were there before the soldiers came are still alive and together.

Before long I start helping the older kids with the chores. Sometimes I tend to the water buffalo. Water buffalo are essential to village life, as they pull the plows that are used to prepare the soil for planting and harvesting the crops.

I also help look after the cows. I wash them and guide their walk and stay with them when they graze. My job is to make sure they don't wander off to another villager's property; otherwise, someone else could claim them. Cows and buffalo are valuable commodities to village life. You wash them and take care of them like they are part of the family.

Another chore I help with is catching fish. When it rains, pools of water form in the low-lying areas. And then after the rain, as the water recedes, you can go into the pool and catch catfish easier, because the water is now shallow.

I join in when it is time to harvest the rice. Initially the rice stems are chopped up into smaller pieces and formed into bundles, which I help carry to a collecting place.

And I dig for water chestnuts. Water chestnuts serve as one of our main food sources during the dry season. Oddly enough, in the dry season rice is scarce, but *water* chestnuts are abundant. Along with walnuts and cashews that you can sometimes find, water chestnuts are our main source of nutrition when there is no fish, chicken, or fowl. There is food to be had in the jungle, but no one dares go in there for it, lest you discover – or are discovered by – a pocket of Khmer Rouge.

For the most part, I just follow after the older kids that are working. If they are busy doing something I can do, I pitch in to help. Either way, they always share their fruit or whatever else they have to eat with me.

About six months after we first arrive at the hut, a frightening thing happens. Out of the blue, one of the 12-year-old boys who lives with us climbs a mango tree and tries to hang himself. And I see it.

I don't realize what he is doing until it is done. Thankfully, Père is able to cut him down before he dies. But the shock and horror of that scene is branded in my mind to this day.

I want Sovannary to share something else with you here because she has some much-needed *good* – and *exciting* – news to tell! She says:

> Not long after leaving my aunt and uncle and returning to the Cambodian camp (I'm now at *Camp Seven*), I meet a high-ranking soldier in the Cambodian resistance. We fall in love and are soon engaged to be married. Yes, even in this surreal context, the normal act of falling in love still happens.
>
> News of our upcoming wedding reaches Aunt Sim, who comes to Camp Seven because she is the only family member available who can oversee my marriage. (It is traditional for a family member to be present to witness a wedding.)
>
> In addition, my fiancé's uncle is very well known throughout the camp, so our wedding becomes quite the event. News of the wedding, along with the fact that I am marrying into a well-known family, spreads deeper into Cambodia. Sidan hears about it.
>
> Upon hearing this news, Sidan decides to leave Sideth with the foster family and escape to the border himself. He is motivated by the same reason I left. He knows that if he stays in Cambodia he and Sideth will soon starve to death.
>
> He also believes that if he can find me now, since I am marrying into a family of means, there may be money enough to buy food to not only save the rest of the foster family but also to get Sideth out of Cambodia. He is thinking correctly, because had he just stayed there, they would likely have both died.

One night Sidan tells Mère and Père that he wants to go to the Thai border. Of course, our new *parents* are worried for his safety (as they had been for Sovannary's), but they understand and are supportive.

Mère has a necklace, twenty-four karat gold. I don't know how she got it, maybe from taking in kids, or in exchange for food that some member of the former upper class needed. Anyway, she cut this necklace in half and gave half to Sidan. She sewed it into the hem of his shirt.

I don't know any of this is going on until Sidan tells me. The news that my brother will be leaving me is just about more than I can bear. It is painful for him too. I see it in his face and hear it in his voice.

51

"I have to leave you. I must go to the border alone because I have more of a chance of making it by myself. When I get to the border, I will get some money. This will allow me to pay for the help I will need to get you out. I will come back for you. I promise I will."

I hurt so bad that I think I am going to die. I am devastated. I bawl until my eyes feel like they will explode out of my head.

I don't think I can live without Sidan. Except for those three months he was in the hospital, he is the only family I have never been without, and the only tether I have left to my real family. I truly don't know if I can go on without him.

I watch him get on that train – not a passenger train but a very old rickety cargo train with a loud, *chooga-chooga-chooga* sound. I chase after that train until it is barely visible. All the while I'm running, I'm crying my eyes out. Just like that, Sidan too has vanished from my life.

An older boy who also lives in the house with our foster family catches up to me. He puts his arm around my shoulder. He holds my hand. He doesn't say anything, but he comes and gets me and takes me back to the house.

I don't eat anything that whole day. I don't want anything to eat. I don't want anything except to go to sleep and forget it all.

The next morning reality hits me hard. Sidan is gone… *really* gone. But I am here, and life goes on. There is nothing left for me to do than consider this family *my family*. So for the next three months…? four months…? five months? I stay here. I don't know how long I am here after Sidan leaves. In one way it seems like forever.

And after a while, once again things fall into a routine of sorts – a kind of *abnormal normalcy*. But life is about to get harder for our makeshift family.

It is the dry season; harvesting is over. All the bags of rice that we once had are now gone – every last one of them. So Mère and Père put all us kids to work gathering food.

Then one day, out of the blue, something very strange happens. About mid-morning, while we are all out in the field foraging, two soldiers walk out of the jungle beyond the rice fields toward us. They are white-skinned, so we know they aren't local and they aren't communist.

They motion for Mère and Père, who stop what they're doing. They all sit down together for a while on the ground and talk. Then the next thing I know, one of the soldiers comes up to me and smiles. He picks me up and puts me on his shoulders. The other soldier joins him and together they take me back to the jungle beyond the rice field.

Oddly enough, I'm not afraid or even curious, to be honest. Truth is, I'm so weak from near starvation that I have no emotional energy to feel anything. Wherever I'm going, I'm going. At this point, it just doesn't really matter.

Once we get beyond the edge of the jungle it's clear this is an encampment of about fifty or sixty soldiers. Not only that, they have stockpiles of food! Bags and bags of rice and loads of other food I don't recognize. They also have guns galore but for some reason, with these soldiers, that doesn't scare me at all.

The soldier lifts me off his shoulders, puts me down, and feeds me a plate of chicken and rice. I have never had chicken before, but boy is it good! I eat and eat. I am so happy, and so are the soldiers watching me.

Once I eat all I can hold, two other soldiers take me to this amazing waterfall and clean me up. When every day is consumed with finding enough food to stay alive that day, regular bathing and general cleanliness are *not* a priority. But this isn't an ordinary bath; we are actually having fun! Those who know how are swimming, and the rest of us enjoy playing in the water together.

Once evening comes and the sun is low in the sky, that same soldier that brought me here puts me back on his shoulders and takes me back to the hut. And when we get there, I see that there are bags of rice that have been brought to us! And a lot of other food too, most of it in cans.

It turns out that while I was away that day, some of the other soldiers bring supplies from their camp in the jungle to my family because they want to help us. What a blessing!

How different a day is when you have enough food to eat! Everybody in our little home is happy again. Now we don't have to continually hunt for food just to stay alive. We go to bed with full bellies and sleep all night, for the first time in a really long time.

A few weeks later in the middle of the night we are all jolted awake by the sound of bombs and gunfire. We think we're being attacked, so everyone jumps up and runs out of the house to these little bunkers – little hills in the rice paddies where you can hopefully hide and be safe. Everybody except me, that is. I am still inside.

For just a few minutes I'm scared to death. But then one of the older girls who lives here comes back for me. She grabs me up and carries me outside to one of the bunkers with her where I see tracer bullets flying in every direction. Exploding bombs billow up past the tops of the trees.

But as it turns out, we are not the target. We just happen to be in the crossfire. The fighting is between the opposition army (the soldiers that helped us) and the communist guerillas.

The fighting goes on for most of the night. Thankfully, by daybreak the jungle is quiet again. So we busy ourselves with the day's chores. It is surreal. Bombing and gunfire at night... chores the next morning.

In the morning, when the temperature is still cool, we feed the animals. I have one cow that I alone am responsible for. My job is to make sure I feed her hay and let her graze the field. Sometimes I ride the cow and even stay with her while she grazes. I know it is important to keep the cow healthy, because without her we have no way to plow the land during the growing season. And without rice, corn, and other vegetables, we will certainly starve.

Farmers do not kill their cows, oxen, or water buffalo for food, unless they just have to. These are working animals, and without them you can't farm. Besides, Asians do not ordinarily eat red meat. Our diet normally consists of fish, chicken, rice, and vegetables.

On a typical day, during the afternoon everyone comes back to the house and helps clean, cook, and eat whatever we gather that day or had saved from the previous day. Then the older boys leave to do more hunting and gathering – mostly looking for fish or any rodents they can find. Even when the lake is bone dry, they can still often find fish somehow. (Our food supply from the opposition soldiers is now gone.)

The dry season is probably the best time to catch fish because it is easier than when the lakes are full. Once the lake is dry, the eels and fish go into hibernation until the rainy season returns.

Another one of my jobs is that of "manager." I watch over the fish the bigger boys catch so the birds don't come and steal them away.

The older girls gather fruits and wild vegetables that are available in the summertime. And then most of what they gather gets preserved in jars. Many of the vegetables are pickled so they will last longer. In fact, I remember eating a lot of pickled mustard greens and cucumbers.

Taro and Lotus root are plentiful options, as well as morning glory, water spinach, bamboo shoots, and different herbaceous plants. As for the fruits, we have mango, sugar palm, lemon, and lime.

After working all day, the younger kids get the evenings free. Most of this time we play games, which I really throw myself into.

One of the games I like watching the older kids play resembles golf. The dirt road is the fairway. Each of the players has a long stick they use as a club. It has to be strong but flexible, and is the length of a baseball bat, though just a bit thinner. A much smaller stick, one that is just a couple of inches long, serves as the "ball" (most often this is a piece of bamboo because bamboo is strong and fibrous).

To tee off, you dig a bit of a hole in the ground and lay the "ball" across the hole sideways. Then you flick the short stick with the long stick. Each person has their own *ball* and *club*, and each takes a turn hitting from the same spot. Whoever flicks the ball the farthest wins.

Sometimes we play hide-and-seek, or just ride bikes around the yard. Only Mère and Père's actual children have bikes. But of course, the kids with bikes share them with the rest of us. I am fascinated with one of the kid's bikes. When you ride the bike, the headlight comes on because of this little motor. The front wheel turns a gear on the motor, which turns on the headlight. We all think that is amazing.

For the most part, despite all the hard times, we are still kids. We don't know enough to be afraid or to worry; we just live in the moment. If there is no imminent threat, we do okay. And if there is a situation that involves some kind of danger, we just do whatever our *parents* tell us to do.

This lack of worry may have been the biggest reason a lot of kids survived this maddening time. Besides, the Khmer Rouge are mainly focused on killing the city people, not us. They would not typically waste a bullet on some kids playing, unless doing so would benefit them in some way.

Despite everything that happened to me in my first six years of life, I believe there is a God. Despite all the evil and killing, loss and devastation, many of the things that occurred when I was without any of my natural family… all point to the existence of a higher, if mysterious, Intelligence. I was too young to realize it then, of course. But I certainly know it now.

One such experience involved me and a rice paddy canal. Rice paddy canals are manmade water-filled canals that run between the rice paddies. These canals serve a few purposes, but the most obvious is to irrigate the rice paddy.

(Cambodia is the world's best at channeling water using irrigation systems that do not involve machines. The ancient city of Angkor was built utilizing such irrigation systems. The city practically floated on water during the rainy season, retaining just enough water to sustain its foundation during the dry season.)

These canals are also very useful for fishing. Fish migrate up and down these canals, burying themselves in the mud during the dry season.

Finally, the canals serve as an opportunity for cooling yourself in the near unbearable heat of Cambodian summers – a heat that can easily climb to over 100 degrees. The high humidity makes it seem even hotter.

One really hot day I watch as some boys run and jump into the canal and swim to the other side. I decide to do the same thing…

Except I don't know how to swim!

My mouth fills up with water. I can't breathe. I bob up and down, maybe three or four times, and realize somewhere in the middle of all this that I am probably about to die. *After all I have lived through… I suffer a simple accident, and I'm done.*

And that's the last thing I remember before losing consciousness.

When I come to, I am somehow back on the bank of the canal, with the rice paddy next to me. As my surroundings are coming back in focus, I see a fisherman walking away from me carrying his fishing pole. I watch as he disappears out of sight. Just like that. Like a dream. I have no idea who he is or what he looks like, other than just a shadow of a person with a fishing pole, walking away.

It reminds me of a passage in the New Testament that says some of us have unknowingly encountered an angel. I wonder now if an angel sometimes comes dressed as a Cambodian fisherman.

I slowly sit up. There's no one around me. No one anywhere. Just the fisherman walking away.

I probably should be scared, but I'm not. I am still groggy and disoriented and too malnourished and exhausted to care about much else. But somehow, I am able to get up on my feet and eventually find my way back to our hut. Back to my second family and the only life I know.

7

The Train, the Pond, and Camp Seven

One very important player in the Ung family story, and my story in particular, is my older brother Sidan. You have already heard a lot about him, but now I would like you to hear *from* him. You can already see why I owe more to him than perhaps anyone else up to this point in my young life, and why I dearly love him.

You have a chance to hear him now, explaining why he chose to leave me with Mère and Père to make for the refugee camp at the Cambodia-Thai border. You will also discover what a harrowing journey that was. He tells us:

> The train is taking its good old time. I crouch by the tracks as low as I can, wondering who's going to get to me first – the train or the Khmer Rouge. All the while the thought repeating in my head is "I hope this works."
>
> Finally, I hear the train. When I see it, my heart sinks a bit. It is just a rickety cargo train, with plain old boxcars full of God knows what. And it's bursting at the seams with people.
>
> The train doesn't stop, but it does slow down. I grab an iron rung when I can and pull myself into the throng.
>
> There are so many people it looks as if they've been stuck onto the train with glue. Everywhere it is possible to do so, a person is wedged. Once I get on, I am able to maneuver myself to the top of the heap where I have a better chance of staying on. What I later

59

realize is that when they see I am just a kid on my own, the adults let me climb on up. That's how I end up on top.

Occasionally someone loses their grip and starts to fall off. They call out for help and thankfully there's always someone close who can lend a hand. We are – after all – all in this together.

We are chugging along at about 10 miles an hour. But even at this pace, the train is still one of the fastest ways to get to the Thai border.

It may not be the safest, however. It is daylight now, so we have less chance of getting shot at by the Khmer Rouge. They mostly come out at night. But at any minute we could get blown up by a bomb dropped by those who think this train belongs to the North Vietnamese. Or the North Vietnamese could bomb it. Or you could just fall off the thing and it's back to thinking about the Khmer Rouge.

I have to pick my poison, and the train seems to be the best choice. And we're all doing it for the same reason – *escape*. There are plenty of other reasons of course – freedom, food, sheer survival. But "escape" sums it all up for me.

There's supposed to be plenty of food at the border. *At least there has to be more there than where I came from*, I think to myself.

I can remember how the three of us – Sovannary, Sideth, and I – struggled to find enough food to survive on before we moved in with our foster family. And I knew it was about to get like that again. I couldn't say that to Sideth, though; I wouldn't want to scare the little guy.

Sideth. It hurt so bad to leave him, but I believe I have to if we are going to survive. I hope someday he'll understand why I had to leave. And I sure hope we both live to talk about it.

I can't let myself think about that right now, however. I must focus on my own survival because if I don't make it, he won't either. As I make myself concentrate on that, the rhythmic *clickety-clack, clickety-clack* of the train feels almost comforting.

Though the train is covered in people, nobody's saying much, only the occasional younger kid asking questions. Although we don't know each other, we do know we're all on the same mission. And we all share the same common suffering.

There's not a lot of empathy between us, however. It is not that we are uncaring; it is just that we are spent from everything we've been through. All the grief and horror and suffering we've experienced to this point consumes us emotionally. We're each just caught up in our own reflections.

It saddens me deeply to think of any child having to grow up so quickly. Even though I'm in the same boat, I am sadder for Sidan than I am for myself because I love him so much.

And maybe it's not that this kind of traumatic life causes a child to *grow up* so quickly. That wording is not quite right. You don't grow up so much as you *grow old* in this kind of setting. And you do so way, way before your time.

But even on that train a Provident hand is looking out for Sidan… greeting him with a tender mercy. He continues:

> Since boarding, I've been able to make three new friends – guys about my age who have the same goal as I do: to get to the Thai border refugee camp. And they know *how* to get there. Or more correctly, one of them does. (Père did what he could to help. He told me which train to take, where it would be headed, and some other good information.)
>
> So there are four of us on this strange adventure, just trying to survive – Pov, Nisay, Makara, and me. (Friendship goes a long way when you're in this situation. Friends in need, friends indeed!)
>
> Pov is a little older than the rest of us, around 17, and he knows a lot more than we do about this trip. Pov says the train is going to stop in Battambang.
>
> "We have to jump off before the train actually goes into the city," he says.
>
> "Why is that?" I ask.
>
> "If you want to live, I suggest you avoid the city; get off and do the rest on foot. The Khmer Rouge control the cities, remember? They'll shoot anyone they catch in the city. This is their supply train. If they see you, you're dead."
>
> That's certainly enough to convince me.
>
> But Battambang isn't close. We keep chugging along for hours… at 10, maybe 15 miles an hour. After a few hours of riding that way you get used to it. It's almost soothing. And we even get a little breeze now and then.
>
> Finally, with the city approaching, we have a decision to make. Once we jump from the train, are we going to stay together or go our separate ways.

"So what do you think, guys?" Makara asks. "Are we gonna stick together?"

"Definitely," Nisay answers.

I agree.

"All right," Pov says. "Ready? One… two… three… *JUMP!*"

"We need to go north," Pov says.

It seems like he knows what he's talking about, so we all agree. "And there's a river on the way."

The river gently flows through the jungle. We dip our hands in… it's nice and cool. And we quench our needy thirst.

And now it's time to cross it. But there's a problem.

"This river's full of man-eating creatures," Nisay says.

"We're going in anyway; we just have to swim fast," says Pov.

I'm not crazy about the idea of man-eating creatures. And I'm certainly afraid of having to swim across a river with them in it!

"We have to get across, that's all there is to it," Pov reasons. "And it doesn't look like there's any alternative to swimming."

We quietly slip into the river. There's nothing to do but to put all your focus and energy into swimming like mad – and trying not to think about being eaten.

We get to the other side and flop on the bank to catch a breather, gather our wits, and talk about what to do next. We're not very far into the conversation before we're all looking at Pov and waiting.

"The Thai border's that way," he says, pointing.

I don't know if he's using any kind of landmarks, has been keeping track of our traverse, or just knows the trail. But you can tell he knows he's right about the direction.

It's about 6:00 or 7:00 in the evening. The sun's about to set. And we all know darkness means even greater danger. We pick the pace up to a jog.

We hear gunshots and it scares us half to death. The soldiers have either seen us or heard us.

"Over there!" we hear one of the soldiers say. *"Quick – over there!"*

We hear more shots, and in rapid succession.

They're not only firing at us; they're now chasing us. Our adrenaline's high, and our speed is unmatched – so far. We grab at trees and swing around them… their thorns and branches digging into our skin.

But they're fast, too. We can hear them behind us; we can hear their voices and other voices on their walkie-talkies.

Our one ally is this – it's getting darker.

Suddenly we see a pond in front of us. In fact, it's now so dark we almost *didn't* see it. The pond is absolutely covered in lily pads, so we can't swim it. Besides, they will catch up with us before we get halfway across.

Pov crouches down at the edge of the pond. He's breaking stems off some kind of plant. He sucks air through it, then blows it out. It's a hollow reed.

We each follow suit and then we all slide into the water as silently as we can. Just before submerging we hear another *CRACK!* from an AK.

I put the reed in my mouth, shut my eyes, and feel the water close over my face. I'm so scared I can hardly relax enough to breath efficiently.

I just hope the evening is now sufficiently dark that they can't see us. *Please God, let it be so.*

I try to focus on not jerking the reed about… and hope the other three are doing likewise.

I just *know* the soldiers are at the edge of the pond looking down into it. And I'm absolutely terrified that I'm going to hear… or feel… a *CRACK!*

And just then several shots from an AK47 rip into the pond. I can only hope they didn't hit one of my mates. Suddenly I am very thankful for the lily pads covering this pond – and for the darkness.

And now there's silence. Minutes that feel like hours pass.

Eventually, I sense movement. I can feel water pulling away from me. One of the others must be surfacing. I make the choice to slowly emerge.

Pov is already standing upright in the water. A minute or so later Nisay quietly stands up. And then Makara. As passively as we possibly can, we move to the other side of the pond and ease out.

Quietly – because we have no idea how far away the soldiers have gone – we begin walking north. For hours. We all feel the need to lie down and rest. We have reached the end of both our courage and our endurance.

As soon as we sit down, someone says something about taking turns standing guard… and that's the last thing I remember.

The next thing any of us know, the sun is up. We don't feel like moving, but we'll need as much daylight as possible in order to get as far as we can. Not even Pov seems to know exactly how much farther we have to go. And the rest of us, of course, are as lost as a bat.

The four intrepid teenagers – it's still hard for me to believe that we're talking about four guys in their mid-teens (Sidan is 15) – travel on through the jungle northward. Eventually they come upon a ragtag *camp* of sorts, with maybe 200 people in it. They discover the place is called Nam Chong, and that it is a holding area for those trying to get to the refugee camp in Thailand.

Sidan starts asking around to see if anyone knows our sister Sovannary. To his surprise – *and relief* – a woman speaks up and says that she does know her! It turns out this woman is one of the traders who goes back and forth between camps. She tells Sidan, "She's in one of those camps near the border, but on the Cambodian side."

"Which camp?" Sidan excitedly asks her. "I need to find her."

The woman's certainty and her quick reply gives Sidan hope. "She's in Camp Seven," the trader tells him.

Sidan says:

I don't think it dawned on me till now just what a long shot this whole thing is. Finding Sovannary has been the driving purpose for my leaving Sideth. I would never have left my little brother for anything else.

I'm thinking that once I find Sovannary, together we can figure out how to get Sideth. We just *have* to figure out how to go back and get him. But I must keep my mind focused on the next step. And right now, I have to get to the border safely and find Sovannary. First things first.

After about a week at Nam Chong, Sidan and his friends head out again for the border. They walk for hours on end.

We have all learned to temper our hope, our expectations, and our anticipations. Too many times, out of nowhere, a crisis appeared that washed away everything bright and positive.

And for the four young travelers, it's about to happen again. Sidan says:

It had to happen, sooner or later. In the dead of night, out of the woods not far from our destination, here come the soldiers. Their guns – always the damn guns – glisten in the faint light of the moon.

One of them speaks. *"MOVE!"* he says to us, indicating the direction with his rifle.

We move. They keep coaxing us forward, along the road.

And then somebody puts a gun to the back of my head. Pov's too. I look sideways and see that the others have guns to their heads also. AK47s, with wooden stocks.

It's strange, the things you notice when there's a gun to your head.

8

Reunion, Joy, Sadness, and Surprise

I'm so glad I didn't know this was happening to my brother. I would have been scared to death. And I would have felt horribly guilty. Here I am in the relative comfort and safety of Mère and Père's hut, surrounded by my surrogate siblings, and my brother has a rifle barrel to his head.

Sidan continues the story for us:

> Though the night air is thick and heavy with heat, the gun metal is ice cold on the back of my head.
>
> *"Where you headed!"* my captor snaps.
>
> "We're going to the camp." I feel pressured to answer quickly. "We're not part of the military," I add. "And we don't have anything." (I had completely forgotten about the gold Mère had sewn into my shirt.)
>
> At some random point they make us stop so they can search each one of us, head to toe. As it turns out, Mère is one heck of a seamstress because they were no more aware of my gold after the search than I was.
>
> Then they take a step back and nod at us. The one in charge says "Okay, you can go."
>
> Our confusion is surpassed only by our relief. We walk on, away from the soldiers. It's takes everything in us not to break into a full-blown run. That might have been okay with our captors... but it might not. And it wasn't worth the risk.

After a while Pov says, "Okay, guys. We have to get off the path. We'll go up the side of that foothill and then turn left about forty-five degrees." This confirms for us something the three of us have suspected from the time we jumped off that train.

Pov has done this before. This has to be the case. He's known everything we've needed to do from the outset. He must be one of the *freedom guides*. We don't ask him to confirm this. We're just grateful to be with him.

"Now for the first thirty minutes, you must be careful. Go as slow as you can without making a sound. When you get down that hill make a run for it, right across the field. Once you do that, you'll see the camp. You can't miss it. Got it?"

"Okay," he says. "Now, good luck – and *let's go!*"

And that's how I learn, beyond the shadow of a doubt, what *running the gauntlet* means.

We do everything Pov says. And when it is time to run, we run for our lives… *literally*… because we are being shot at.

Thankfully, my brother and his friends survive the gauntlet! Not only that, but they are now at their long-sought destination. They are at Camp Seven.

Sidan is thinking, "*My sister is supposed to be here. This is where she was headed when she left our foster family months ago, and I've got to find her.*"

As before, Sidan calls out our sister's name as he walks, looking everywhere. He asks everyone he meets if they know her.

Eventually his persistence pays off.

"Yes, I know her," says a woman Sidan describes as looking about as friendly as one of the soldiers back in the jungle.

Sidan responds excitedly, "You've seen her? *Sovannary Ung?*"

Sidan picks up the story:

"What do you have to trade?" she asks me. "Do you have anything to trade?"

"No, lady, I don't have anything. I just got here. I just want to know if you have seen Sovannary Ung?"

"You have *nothing?*" she asks.

"Look… when I find her, I will find you and I will give you whatever I have. But first I need to find her."

"Next time I see you, you better have it then." She adds, "Your sister is married now – to a soldier who is pretty high ranking. Go that way, about a hundred meters."

"Thanks!" (I don't tell her that the whole reason I'm here is because I know my sister is now married.)

"You can't miss them... and don't forget – you owe me!"

I walk faster now, all the while continuing to call her name. Suddenly I am surprised by a warmly familiar voice.

"*Sidan!*"

As soon as I see Sovannary, my first thought is that she's awfully thin. And she looks so tired... even more so than when she left, as I remember.

"*Sovannary!*" I say her name for the millionth time today, only now she's right here, right in front of me. I can hardly believe it! We run to each other and hug as never before. And cry... hard. Then we hug some more.

It's almost too much to believe that, after everything we've each been through, we have finally found one another!

Then it hits me like a jolt when she asks, "*Where's Sideth?*"

It's a perfectly fair question. It's the right question. *The main question.* There's only one answer to it. And yet it's the hardest question I ever had to answer.

"He's... I had to leave him."

The color goes out of her face. "What?" She can only manage a whisper. Her eyes fill with water.

I look away. I feel an overwhelming sense of guilt for leaving him behind. I feel responsible for the pain and sorrow so evident on Sovannary's face.

"Sideth's not here."

I'm feeling sick. And I know she is too.

"I don't understand..."

"He was in no condition to come with me. He's still at the foster parents' house."

She closes her eyes. "Thank God! I thought you were going to tell me he was..."

"Dead? Oh no, he's with them!"

"*Oh, thank God!*" She hugs me tight. I feel her sobbing.

Instantly, I know what I have to do. I have to turn around tomorrow and go back. You don't leave your brother behind – and I should have known that.

"I'm going back for him tomorrow."

"What?"

"I said I'm going back for him tomorrow."

"I heard what you said. *But you can't.*"

Maybe she's trying to make me feel less guilty, and I appreciate that. But it's the right thing to do. I'm *sure* of it. I have to.

"But you just got here!"

"Yeah… I just had to make sure you were okay."

"You're not making sense."

"Sure I am. Look, Sis. I messed up."

"No, no, no. Look… *I* left – I left you *both*. I *had* to… for the same reasons *you* did. You couldn't bring him. And he's in better hands right now."

"It's no excuse. I should've brought him. I can do it."

"You're not thinking it through." She shakes her head furiously, closing her eyes like she's shaking out tears. "You won't be that lucky again. And you *certainly* can't do it with a little kid on your back the whole time."

She might have a point, but I don't care.

"Are you sure he's even alive?"

Of course, I'm not sure. No one ever knows if anyone's alive anymore. Which is why I never asked myself that question the whole time I was running. "How can you ask me that?"

"Because I can't lose my last brother, that's why."

I can't think in those terms. Not when I'm the one that left Sideth back there. I can't bring myself to consider what she's saying.

"Yes," I tell her. "The answer to your question is *yes*. I mean, he was alive when I left him. But they were running out of food… which is why I have to go *tomorrow.*"

"Sidan, are you even listening to me? You won't be that lucky twice, especially with a kid on your back. I can't let you risk losing your life too. We'll just have to figure something out."

At that moment a couple of kids about Sideth's age run in front of us, laughing. I can't bear to look at them.

Reunited, brother and sister walk together around the camp. Sovannary says, "I wish Aunt Sim was still here. She would know what to do."

Assuming the worst, Sidan thinks she is saying that Aunt Sim has been killed. For the first time in forever, Sovannary chuckles.

"Oh no! She's fine! They made it to Thailand. In fact, their whole *family* did. Can you believe it?"

This somehow makes Sidan even lonelier for me.

Sometimes we have an experience that makes us feel so loved, so valued, that it overwhelms us. Sidan is on the verge of just such an experience, and Sovannary is its source. I'll let her share it with you as she continues the conversation with Sidan:

> "In fact, I made it to Thailand, too."
>
> "You did? Well, yeah, I guess you *would* have… I mean, if you're saying *they* did. It makes sense that you'd know that because you were there too. So, why in God's name did you come back *here?*"
>
> "Because I couldn't leave without you and Sideth."

Sidan regains his composure. Not knowing what to say in the face of such an overwhelming gift of love, he decides to change the subject.

"So, you're married?" he says to our sister.

Sidan quietly thinks to himself, "How is it possible that life manages to keep getting stranger?" Ironic, because he's not at all ready for the *one up* he's about to be hit with – a one-up that only goes to further prove his thought correct.

"Not only that… I'm going to have a baby!"

9

He's Not Here Yet, Is He?

In a day full of surprises, Sidan is about to be hit with another one. He has just heard the news that, not only is our sister now married, but he and I are going to be uncles! As brother and sister walk, they see a visitor who has come to the camp – expected by the sister, unexpected by the brother. It was our aunt, Sim Long.

She screams with joy when she sees Sidan! After handing Sovannary a bag full of vegetables and canned goods, she starts the same hugging-and-crying ritual Sidan and Sovannary have just finished. Then she speaks those maternal words, *"How you've grown!"* followed by *"You've got to eat something!"*

We are fortunate in that we have Sidan's own words to share with us the exchange that followed:

> While Aunt Sim wipes tears of joy from her eyes, she says, "Well, that's two now."
>
> "How many bullets did you dodge just to check on me this time?" my sister asks.
>
> "What? None," she answers lovingly.
>
> Turning toward me, Sovannary explains, "Our Aunt… she holds the record for most frequent visitor, you know."
>
> "I have to make sure you're okay," my aunt says, smiling.

But then her smile wavers and fades. "So, my baby's not here yet, is he." It's more of a statement than a question; she can sense it. "He's not sleeping in your tent."

"No." I let Sovannary say it.

Our aunt looks at me, sadly, but not unkindly, which is a small consolation but a welcome relief. She makes me feel like I'm standing in the warm glow of her love, regardless of what I did or didn't do in this world. I may not be the most expressive person, but I can tell you I needed that from her at that moment. I need the love and understanding of both Aunt Sim and Sovannary right now, simply because I'm beating myself up for deciding to leave Sideth behind.

She has a million questions for me, though I don't hear most of them because it's hard for me to think about much else, other than my little brother.

Sovannary tells Sidan that Aunt Sim knows all about what has happened to our family. She informed our aunt and uncle when she first met up with them some time back.

Sidan remembers being grateful for that. Feeling so low about having to leave me behind, he didn't feel he had the heart or energy to recount all our family losses to her.

And then Aunt Sim gave Sidan another one of those priceless gifts:

"I'm so sorry. What else can I say? Your family was our family – and the three of you left are now so, more than ever. You don't know how it hurts me for them... and for you. But we're here now." She hugs me again. "I'm just so relieved you're with us again!"

And then once again, in true maternal style she says to my brother, *"And you need to wash and eat!"*

Our sister informs Sidan that Aunt Sim has been running the gauntlet between the camp in Thailand (Khoa-I-Dang) where she and her family now live, and the camp Sovannary, and now Sidan, are in. She adds that our aunt does this on a regular basis.

Then again Sidan is given one of those gifts that shows there are still people in this sad world we're in that love him... that love the three of us. Sovannary says, "She does this just to make sure I am okay... and to see if there's any word about you and Sideth."

We are the reason our courageous and loving Aunt Sim continues to risk her life by leaving the safety of Khoa-I-Dang and traveling the dangerous gauntlet to this camp. "And she keeps bringing me food and money," Sovannary adds.

Their conversation continues – and on a funny note. But then matters turn serious… deadly serious. Sidan says:

> After Sovannary's comment about the food and money Aunt Sim says "And your sister is here because she decided to get married. In a refugee camp, no less! She did tell you that, didn't she?"
>
> "I did," Sovannary chimes in.
>
> "In a refugee camp," Aunt Sim repeats – with an impish smile as she shakes her head.
>
> "You never know what tomorrow will bring," Sovannary responds.
>
> "True," says Aunt Sim.
>
> She looks around and shakes her head. "This place…" And then she looks at me and adds… "You be careful."

> The next thing we know, our shared lunch is interrupted by a great many people yelling, *"RUN!"* And I soon realize why. I hear the whistle of bombs, a sound we all know too well.
>
> There's a mad rush, everyone heading in the same direction. Sovannary reaches for my hand. I grab it and Aunt Sim grabs my other one.
>
> One thing I'm quickly learning – this camp is not a good place to be. And it's dangerous. It may be a step up from the workcamps, but that's about all I can give it.
>
> And when Aunt Sim said to be careful, she wasn't even talking about the bombings. She's referring to the shootings that occur right here, on the *inside*, just about every day. The place is basically a free-for-all. People daily get killed for money or for food. They get killed *by* thieves… and *for* thieving. There are no rules here. Everything is done black-market style.
>
> And rape is as common as theft.
>
> If you ask me, people as bad as the Khmer Rouge are everywhere; they're just not as organized. So yes… this isn't a workcamp and it isn't the jungle. But it's not a good place to be either.

Experiences like this bombing raid are as surreal as they are terrifying. One minute a ragtag collection of people just trying to survive and make it to safety are sitting at their hut and talking. The next thing, they are running for their lives.

Within just minutes after it begins, families are seeing to their dead and wounded, then sit together and grieve. Those fortunate enough to have survived help out or return to their simple, almost subhuman lives.

There is a line from a famous movie that says, *"Hell is the absence of reason."* Helpless people being bombed just for the evil doing of it, qualifies as some circle of hell, by that definition.

Sovannary tells Aunt Sim of Sidan's intent to make the dangerous journey back for me the next day. I suspect one of her motives is to enlist our aunt's aid in talking him out of it.

Her efforts pay off... or at least they buy some time. Aunt Sim tells Sidan that he should wait a few days to rest, eat, and build his strength back up. To Sovannary's welcomed relief, he agrees to this.

The next morning over a breakfast of fruit and a little fish, Sidan hears the best news he's heard in... well, who knows how long! Let's listen in on their conversation. The point of view is that of Sidan:

> Aunt Sim says "We are leaving. All of us. I don't know where we are going yet but it will be somewhere in the new world. France, the United States, Canada. I don't know... just somewhere away from here. Don't worry. Your uncle is working on it."
>
> She adds, "But in the meantime, we have to get Sideth here, to *this* camp."
>
> *"I* have to get him here. It's *my* responsibility," I say.
>
> "For the last time, Sidan... *no,*" our aunt says firmly. It's clear that now she's completely on Sovannary's side. Then she adds, "But I know how we're going to do it." Sovannary looks as surprised as I do.
>
> *"We?"* I ask her. "We're *all* going?"
>
> Aunt Sim laughs. "Oh, no! I'm going to pay someone."
>
> "Who?"
>
> Sovannary looks at me. "Aunt Sim knows everyone here. Did she tell you that?"
>
> "She's exaggerating, of course," says our aunt. "But there has to be someone we can trust here, as long as the price is right – it's going to cost a pretty penny."
>
> Then all of a sudden it hits me. "Wait a minute," I said. "I have gold!"

They stare at me, both of them, like I'm still delirious from starvation. Then Aunt Sim says, *"Shh!"* and puts her hand on my shoulder.

"Okay," I whisper. I feel the little gold pieces in the seam of my shirt. They're still there! Aunt Sim feels them and nods as if she knows exactly how much there is… and what it's worth. In fact, I have no doubt she does.

"Mère, our foster mother – gave me half a necklace when I left. She told me it was 'twenty-four karat gold,' whatever that means. She gave it to me in case I needed it to bargain for my life or something."

I start to remove the gold and Aunt Sim quickly stops me. She ushers us to a place where people won't see.

"Lesson number one…" my aunt says, "be cautious, be smart."

She feels the part of my shirt where Mère had sown in the gold to hide it. She starts to undo the thread, which causes the little gold pieces to fall into her hand. I welcome the chance to part with it for Sideth's sake. Somehow I think this is the safest place in Cambodia to barter with the gold that will get my brother back.

"That's gold, all right!" my aunt confirms. Then she holds my face in her hands and kisses me on both cheeks. "Sidan, you're a fine young man; you're going to save your brother's life. But I'm pretty sure we're going to need more. Let's see what we have."

Aunt Sim lets out a heavy exhale. "Okay. Not bad."

"I have some jewelry," my sister adds.

"I'm going back to Khoa-I-Dang to bring back some more," says Aunt Sim. She looks worried, like she's concerned we're running out of time.

"Are you sure?" Sovannary says. There's a plea in her voice.

"Yes. We're going to need more. I better get going, *now*. You two stay here and I'll be back in a few days."

I'm convinced Aunt Sim knows what she's doing. She'll find the right person for the job.

Even so, at that moment a horrible picture crosses my mind – of Sideth and that poor family, down to their last meal… and maybe soldiers…

But I dismiss it, while at the same time my aunt pushes her own worried expression away with a smile.

"Okay," Sovannary says, sadly. "But even if we have all the money, I still can't imagine who on earth is going to make that trip."

> "*I'll tell you who.*"
>
> It's a soft, deep voice… and it didn't come from any of us.
>
> That was my introduction to my sister's husband, my brother-in-law, the soldier. His name is Ny Keo. (Pronounced just like Nike, the sports company.)
>
> "Who?" Sovannary asks him.
>
> "Don't ask," Ny Keo says quietly. "But trust me when I tell you he's the right man for the job. And with everybody pitching in, there'll be enough to pay him."

Thankfully, Sovannary is able to describe in excellent detail *generally* where our foster family lives. She describes the hut, the covered well, the mountains in the back…

And most importantly, she is able to describe what the little fella – yours truly – looks like that answers to the name *Sideth*.

Sidan continues:

> I discover how it is that Sovannary feels somewhat safe in this crazy place. I learn that Ny Keo is part of the group – whoever they are – that's more-or-less trying to run the camp. One thing we do know, these people are against the Khmer Rouge. But oddly, according to Sovannary, sometimes they work with the Thai, and sometimes they fight them. Just more of the strangeness of life in Cambodia at this time.

What no one in my little family group there at the border knew at that time is that, as hard as it is to believe, there is another danger in play. And this one is intimate. Personal. Somebody in the camp's ruling hierarchy wants Ny Keo dead.

PART 2

10

Hard Decisions Driven by the Heart

Aunt Sim is *such* a big player in our narrative at this time. There is absolutely no telling how our story would have turned out without her. My heartfelt belief is that, whatever the outcome, it wouldn't have been good.

I'm going to let her speak to you at length in this chapter. She provides essential material about a critical juncture in our story. Not only that, I want you to get a glimpse into the character of the strong, courageous woman that is my Aunt Sim Long.

She says:

> Khoa-I-Dang, the refugee camp in Thailand, is a lot nicer than the Cambodian camps. It is cleaner, better organized, and has enough food and shelter for everyone. It even has running water! The shelters are made of bamboo and thatch, and actually resemble huts lined up in neat rows like barracks.
>
> The camp where Sovannary and Sidan are staying [Camp Seven] is, by contrast, so overcrowded there is never enough of *anything*. The shelters, if you can call them that, are made of anything that can be thrown together.
>
> Another difference is that the Khoa-I-Dang camp is run by official international charity groups like UNICEF, the Red Cross, and the World Food Program. They have the backing of the United States and the United Nations. As a result, Cambodian refugees are getting sponsored daily, allowing them to leave Khoa-I-Dang for better futures in other countries.

No matter how horrible the living conditions are in the Cambodian camp, however, after learning that Sidan made it safely, I seriously considered staying with them until I know Sideth is also here safe. After all, they are my family too, and they need me.

But I'm deeply torn. My husband and children are back in Khoa-I-Dang, and they need me too. So as hard as it is for me to say goodbye to Sovannary and Sidan, I know I have to go.

When I get back to Khao-I-Dang, I am met with some surprising news.

"We've been selected!" Kari, my husband, calls to me. He is so happy. He walks quickly toward me, with arms outstretched, as soon as he sees me.

"Selected for what?" I ask.

"What do you think... *to go to America!* A bus will take us from here to another camp, Chon Bouri, where they get us ready to go to the United States. Look, we don't have much time. You've got to get Sovannary. Pay whoever you need to bring her here right away, because there's no telling...." Noticing my lack of enthusiasm, he interrupts himself. "What's wrong? Aren't you happy?"

"What? Of course, I'm happy!" *America! Freedom!*

Those two words – *America* and *freedom* – had been linked in our heads ever since we knew that, to survive, we had to get out of here and start a new life.

"Then... what's the matter with you?"

I try to compose myself while hiding my concerns. But in my heart, I know I can never leave Sovannary and Sidan – and especially Sideth – in Cambodia. After all, they lost all their family... and these are my sister's children.

So I change the subject. "Sidan's back."

Now it's Kari's turn to be stunned. He's happy, too, of course – almost in tears, in fact. But there are other emotions warring for attention, and it's all over his face.

"Sidan made it?" he asks. Then, quietly, shaking his head, "That poor family."

"That's *our* family," I say.

"I know!" There is a twinge of defensiveness in his voice. But that fades quickly and is replaced by deep sorrow in his eyes.

"I know," I repeat for him. I want – *need* – to say a lot more, obviously.

"Well," after a bit of a pause, "we better start getting ready," Kari says. "When it's time, we have to be ready to go."

Aunt Sim and Uncle Kari are soon told that they have two weeks to get ready to leave the refugee camp in Thailand. Just two weeks and they will be leaving the years of this ordeal behind them!

Thankfully, the process for departure is easy compared to all they've gone through to get to that point. Basically, it's a matter of showing up on time at the prescribed date and answering a few questions. In fact, little more than the names and ages of the members of your family are required.

A word of explanation is useful here. Once a family is given sponsorship, the intended process is to give them two weeks to get ready to report. But an operation this big, in a region of the world this chaotic, is often beyond the bounds of clockwork precision. It could just as easily be that you receive word in five days, or seven, or ten that the timetable has shifted, and you have to go *now*. And it's just as likely that something occurs causing a family to get bumped backward... delayed. More uncertainty!

Aunt Sim picks up the story:

> I should be happy. Who wouldn't be happy to see the light at the end of this tunnel? A chance to get out of this ugly situation... a chance for you and your husband and all your children to start over in a place where people are free and can actually lead happy lives? Based on everything we have heard about America, we *know* that's where we want to be. And now that our chance is finally here... I know I should be thrilled.

> But I'm not. What before was an incredible opportunity for our family now feels like an ultimatum. I now have a responsibility that I can't ignore, one that I can't just shrug off or pass along to someone else.

> No one in my family – not even Kari – has any idea how heavily this responsibility is weighing on me. My sister is gone, and I must pick up where she left off. I am responsible to take care of her children now. That's how mothers – and sisters – are.

> And Sideth? There's no way I can put into words what I feel for that baby. It's ripping my heart out, knowing that he's still inside Cambodia. But unlike his brother and sister who's just across the border from us, we have no idea where. All I know is that we only have two weeks to find him and bring him here.

For most people waiting to go to America, two weeks would seem like forever. As for me... I'm grateful it's two instead of one. And who knows? Two weeks still may not be enough time.

And what if we're called up earlier than two weeks? They could call us at any time. If a slot opens in the schedule and they decide to give it to us, we have to be ready to go.

I also know, however, that I can't leave without Sideth. And that's just the way it is. Besides, I'm the only one in a position to try to get him back. Kari is a doctor in Khao-I-Dang, and everyone else in the family, well, they're children.

Not only that, I have the will... and the means – with a little help from Sidan and Sovannary and Sovannary's husband. But now that I'm back in Khao-I-Dang and have time to consider everything we're up against, I begin to have doubts. Who knows whether this guy Ny Keo selected has even left yet? Or if he even cares about the wellbeing of a child? How do we know he won't simply take the money and run?

Ny Keo assured us that he is the right person for the job. And although I don't know Ny Keo very well, he seems trustworthy. Not only that, I'm sure he wants Sideth back safely too, for Sovannary's sake if nothing else. It's clear he's crazy about her and wants to protect her. Getting Sideth here safe is one way he can protect her from further heartbreak.

"So, you'll be ready?" my husband asks. "Everyone will be ready, right?" I don't know if he means to include Sidan or not. And I am afraid to ask. But I can't avoid his question any longer, so I break down and tell him I'm not going. "If you can't get two more names added to the list, then I won't be going."

"*Two* names?" he asked. "Sovannary *and* Sidan?"

"Sidan and Sideth."

"Sideth is *gone*." Kari really is sorry. But as a doctor, he is also a realist. He is ready to face the fact that our little nephew is almost certainly dead... and ready to do what is necessary to protect his own family.

But I can't settle for that. I can't allow myself to agree with him. I tell him that when Sidan left Sideth he was alive, and that we had gathered our money and paid someone on the other side to go deep into the country and get him.

"I *have* to wait for him."

"You don't know..."

"I know my gamble is a huge risk, but it's a risk worth taking. And I also know that if I don't try, I won't be able to live with myself."

We argue back and forth for a while, but he is determined to leave with the family as soon as they call our names.

I finally have to just tell him point blank, "If you can't get two more names added, you'll have to go on to America with our kids and I will meet up with you later." At least I was *hoping* I would be able to meet up with them later.

He said nothing for the next few minutes.

"*Two* more names? *That's* what you're asking for?"

It's hard to imagine the pressure all of this is adding to an already stretched-to-the-limit stressful situation. My uncle has finally managed to get his family in a place and in a circumstance where they will be able to soon leave this madness. That has been his and our aunt's consuming thought every minute of every day – *for years*.

And now with Sidan having appeared and new information about me having come to light, Aunt Sim is persuaded to the depths of her heart and resolute in her will that she will not leave unless her nephews – her new children – are with them.

Though truly sorry about our plight, Uncle Kari cannot believe his wife is willing to risk the freedom and wellbeing of their family to see to us. Aunt Sim can't believe he doesn't understand why she can't leave us behind. Now personal tension *within* their family is added to the pressures already facing them.

My cousin, Malis (oldest daughter of Uncle Kari and Aunt Sim), sheds some firsthand light on this stressful time:

> I overhear Mother telling Father that she is not leaving without Sideth. After she tells him, there is a long silence.
>
> Of all our cousins, Sideth is her favorite. We all know that. Without question she loves Sidan and Sovannary as well – but Sideth is her pick. (I suspect this is because he is the baby of my now deceased Uncle Neak and Aunt Kim's almost extinct family.)
>
> After that initial conversation, Mother and Father continue in heated – though usually private – discussions for days. Mother doesn't talk to Father for a while, and it's clear that Father is mad, too.

"Are you willing to throw away your children's future for this?" he asks Mother. "You don't know where Sideth is... or if he's even alive. And if he is alive now, what are the odds of some stranger risking their life to get him delivered to us without them both being killed?" Yet nothing Father could say is strong enough to convince Mother to change her mind.

"I'm not going to America. You are free to take our children and go and I... *we* will join you when we can. But I have to wait for Sideth. I have to wait until I get him back here with me."

Hearing this breaks my heart to the point of tears. More than anything else, I want our family to get to go to America together. But in my mother's eyes, we are *all* – the nine of us and the three of them – *one* family. And I think she is right.

If I'd had any idea about how unlikely the chance was that Sideth would make it safely to the border... or the narrow time frame available to get him here... I would be a lot more upset than I am. I simply hope they work this out and that everything turns out okay. The best I can do is hope they find a way to make it work.

Of course, the last thing Father wants is to leave Mother. Our family was separated for *four years* while the Khmer Rouge were looking to kill Father. All that time, we didn't know where he was or if he was even still alive.

We just recently reunited, so the idea of being separated again – especially so soon – is just too hard to accept.

But I hear Mother tell him, "You need to go to whoever put the application in for you and tell them to add two more names."

That's my mother; when she wants something, she won't let it go until she gets it.

"Well, as much as I'd like to, I cannot do that. What's done is done. You know how it works... you just accept what you've been given and know how fortunate you are to get it."

Everyone seems to understand that but Mother. And she's not budging.

As for me, I don't think there was a right or wrong answer regarding all of this. Aunt Sim is showing the fierce love of a Mother's heart toward Sovannary, Sidan, and me in her decision not to leave without us. Still, I can see how some reading this story will think this was unwise of her.

Uncle Kari is showing a husband and father's strong desire to protect his family and keep them together. I can see why some reading this would think he is being calloused about the plight of his niece and nephews.

But as I said, for me it's not a matter of which is right and which is wrong. Instead, given their perspective and vantage point, each is right.

I learned at an early age never to say, "It can't get any worse," or "This is as bad as it can get." As anyone who lived in Cambodia during the years of the civil war can tell you, it can *always* get worse… or stranger… or sadder… or more difficult.

My older brother Sidan illustrates my point from a conversation between he and Sovannary that was happening concurrently with tension between our aunt and uncle:

> I say to my sister, "Sovannary, it's going to be great when Sideth gets here and we can all go to America."
>
> To my shock… and horror, I hear her say, "I'm not going."
>
> *"What?"*
>
> "I'm not going." She looks down at the ground and shakes her head.
>
> "You're kidding, right?"
>
> "No… but I don't expect you to understand."
>
> "Well, you're right. I don't! But nothing makes sense anymore."
>
> "I wanted to tell you when Aunt Sim was here."
>
> "She knows this?"
>
> "Yes. And she gets it."
>
> "Well, let's talk about it when she gets here then, because I want to hear it from her. There's no way you're going to make me understand. This sounds crazy to me."
>
> Sovannary starts crying. I try to comfort her. I don't understand what she is saying to me at all, but the last thing I want is to make her cry.
>
> "My *new* family's here. That's why," she says, through tears.
>
> I still don't understand. Not really. But it's clear Sovannary has made up her mind and nothing I can say will make any difference.

The tension is mounting as the time is drawing nearer. The two weeks are just about up. How quickly the days are passing!

Aunt Sim says:

It's more than just a hop, skip, and a jump between camps. There are about 14 kilometers (almost 9 miles) of bullet-infested jungle joining Khoa-I-Dang to the Cambodian camp – Camp Seven.

But with only three days left before we are scheduled to leave for the U.S., I leave Khoa-I-Dang and cross back to Camp Seven. They obviously haven't called us up yet. And that is good. *Please God don't let them.*

Please God...

11

A Long and Dangerous Bike Ride

Months had passed since Sidan hopped the train for the border. As much as it broke my heart to watch the last connection to my real family fade into the distance, at least I was in a foster family with a father and mother who loves me, protects me, and tries their best to keep me enough food to eat.

Then one day, out of the blue, Père asks me if I want to go for a ride on the bike. He has the bike ready for us to leave when he asks me. The bike is old, brownish and rusty in color, and has a bucket-type metal seat on the back.

Mère is standing there with us when he asks me. Before I can even answer him, she picks me up, gives me a huge hug, and sits me down in the seat. She then smiles at me, and with tears in her eyes holds my face in her hands, gives me a big kiss on the cheek, looks me in the eye, and tells me she loves me.

In and of itself, this is nothing unusual. Mère is always that way – warm and affectionate – showing and sharing how much she loves us. But this time, as soon as she says so, she hurries away and goes back into the hut. Her behavior seems a little strange, but so does this sudden idea of a bike ride with my father that came out of nowhere.

Before I can wonder too much about what is going on, however, Père mounts the bike and we take off. He's pedaling fast, so fast in fact that I have to hold on tight with both arms around his waist just to hang on.

"That's it – hold on, son."

I think, "okay," though for some reason I don't say it out loud. But that's not so unusual these days. In fact, I don't talk a lot or do much else that takes energy because I'm always tired.

I have no idea where we are going, or why. All I know is that I was placed on a bike, and off we went. At first, I thought Père was just taking me for a bike ride through the countryside. But the longer we go, the less I understand what we're doing. Every now and again I steal a glance back at our hut, which is farther and farther away each time. And then, before I know it, I look back and our house is nowhere in sight.

I'm thinking, "Okay, that's enough riding. I'm tired and I want to go home now." But I don't say anything because I can somehow tell that this isn't part of the plan. The longer we ride, the clearer it is that this is no ordinary bike ride. With home so far behind us now that it is out of sight, I'm sure wherever Père's taking me, it's not just for a bike ride. And somehow, I have this feeling that I will never be going back.

After we've been riding at this frenetic pace for a couple of hours, maybe more, I desperately need to stop. My stomach is hurting, nature is calling, and I can't keep ignoring it. No matter what else is going on, after a while these normal functions have a way of getting your attention.

I'm about to ask Père if we can take a break, but then something stops me. He looks quickly from one side to the other, and then back again. It's obvious he's on a mission – and it's clear there's a lot at stake. You can tell by how it feels (every refugee knows that feeling).

Even I can tell he's not hurrying for nothing. He is *scared*. Wherever we're going, we just have to *go*. And we have to get there *fast*.

So I decide to say nothing about my need to stop.

We're now riding through rice paddies bordering the rolling bright green countryside. It feels to me like we are the only two people on the planet. No one is on this dirt road but Père and me. Everything around us is quiet and calm, interrupted only by a welcome breeze every now and again. In the late afternoon sun, the sky proudly presents more reds and oranges than I've ever seen in one place. The whole countryside is radiant with a strange beauty and even a magical feel about it. It's like a serene, pastoral painting that I'm in the middle of.

Regardless of the strange nature of this journey, the world from this perspective is all new to me. With the sun beaming down, the sky on fire, the lush green of the country, the blazing gold of the rice paddy… it's mesmerizing. I have never seen the world this way. It seems like I've never had the chance to stare at it all for this long… and let my mind wander along with it.

After several hours of moving at such a hurried pace, the evening breeze makes it seem like the perfect time to take a nap. I don't think Père will mind. By now I'm convinced he doesn't need me to do anything anyway. Everything is so peaceful in fact, that I even forget about my need to make a bathroom stop.

While I'm mostly numb to it by now, this mysterious, confusing trip doesn't fit any definition of the word *comfortable*. The dirt road we're on is nothing more than a footpath several feet wide at best, certainly not wide enough to accommodate anything more than a bike.

Navigating the rocky path is clearly challenging for Père. In fact, I'm afraid that if I move around or shift my weight or make any sort of adjustment in my seat, we will surely both flip over and tumble right smack into the muddy rice paddy.

Every now and then Père asks me if I'm okay. That's about all the talking there is on this strange trip.

Day turns into evening, and the rice paddies turn into jungle. One minute I'm looking at the sun setting low over the paddies, and the next thing I know we're hidden in the thick darkness of the rain forest.

The road through the jungle is riddled with potholes and tree roots. My bony bottom is getting terribly sore from bouncing around for hours in this metal seat. And I'm having another problem. It's getting harder and harder to ignore this much needed and long-overdue call of nature. But I still don't ask Père to stop.

Given the laws of biology however, eventually the inevitable happens. It doesn't matter that we are deep in the jungle and trying to get… *somewhere*… as fast as we can. I simply can't hold it in anymore. And the next bump we hit is the proverbial camel's straw.

The nature of this trip being what it is, I just have to sit in it. I know by Père's behavior that we can't afford even a minute's break. We can't just stop and relax and wash up at will.

But at some point, I suppose he can't stand the smell any longer... not to mention the flies we are now attracting. So at the next sight of water, Père jolts to a stop, whisks me off the seat, dunks me in and out of the water enough times to count for a washing, splashes some in my seat to complete the job, and we're off again.

With my bottom washed but still wet, I drift off to sleep... briefly. On waking I find that the air is a bit cooler now, though still thick with humidity, and that the sun has gone to sleep. I wake up to realize how hungry and thirsty I am... and that I'm still on the back of this bike.

Thoughts of my hunger and thirst are interrupted with unnerving sounds of the night – birds and monkeys screeching from random directions. In fact, it seems every animal in the jungle is screeching and screaming over something. In my child's mind I imagine that they are all talking to each other.

I suddenly realize that up to now I've enjoyed a certain sense of safety, riding on the back of the bike with my père at the wheel. But that feeling is quickly giving way to those of fear and pending danger.

The path through the jungle is a little wider now, with other people coming and going. Some are traveling the same direction as we, while others are going the other way. Where they are coming from, or going to, I don't know.

But what I do know is that some of these people have guns and they will kill you for reasons no one understands. I also realize that whatever we're trying to accomplish puts us in the category of people they don't like. Even as a six-year-old kid, I know this trip is as likely to end badly as it is to end well.

There's nothing more to do now but keep moving. I realize that much, even in my young mind. I just wish I knew where we're going. Or why.

The long ride continues. Night gives way to daylight, but little else changes. Again, we ride all day. I feel as if I'm in a trance. And my legs are numb.

Once the sun begins to set again, however, Père stops quite unexpectedly. He gets me off the bike and sits me down on the ground right next to him. Then without saying anything, he pulls out some rice that he has packed in a can – a regular tin can like you buy tomato soup in at the grocery store.

Other people that appear to be going to the same place we are have also stopped here. Like us, they look half terrified and completely exhausted. But it's clear we're all in the same boat, so someone close by offers to share their fire with us. Père cooks a couple handfuls of rice for each of us. It's not enough to satisfy the hunger pangs, but it will keep starvation at bay.

Night envelops us again, and soon the monkeys and birds resume their conversations. Despite the noise however, I fall asleep in the jungle up against a tree and next to Père. He is now the only constant in my life.

The sun rises, and we with it. So far, I have not complained once about this impossible, bizarre trip. I think it's largely because I'm so weak from malnutrition that I have nothing to complain with. I feel barely alive.

Père isn't doing much better. Thankfully he musters enough strength, perhaps fear-driven strength, to keep going.

The next thing I know we're on the bike again, chugging along kind of slowly now. I'm so hungry and thirsty. It never goes away. It's always sitting there in my stomach. The thirst is getting worse, though. What's ironic is that water is everywhere in the jungle, but you don't dare wander off the path for fear of who you might encounter.

The trees hover low over the dirt road, like arms that want to hug it. And the road we're on now is a lot wider and looks like it's used a lot. You can even see car tracks and motorcycle tracks, in addition to the bike tracks. At least for now, this part of the road is a lot smoother than it was on the first days of our journey, and my backside appreciates it.

We continue until the sun drops over the horizon again. But since we're in the jungle, it seems like night. The air is thick and heavy. And there's a distinct smell now, like something dead… animals, or maybe even people. It's strong, which means there's a lot of them.

With night comes the familiar screeching and screaming of the animals. It sounds for all the world like they are all arguing with each other now. These noises follow us for miles. At some point I hear a crow calling out. In my imagination I hear him saying, "Go back! Go back!"

There's also the sound of a rifle – no doubt, the dreaded AK47. How sad that we're all so use to it, and so exhausted, that nobody seems to even notice. But me. I notice.

Since Père just keeps peddling, I do nothing more than casually say to myself, "It's just another gun going off." It doesn't happen often, thank goodness. But when it does it's always followed by dead silence. Even the animals go quiet. Then a minute later they all start up again. It's like the jungle is trying to tell us something, but we keep ignoring it.

As it gets darker, we slow down. At this pace the mosquitoes and gnats do with us what they will. The mosquitoes in this part of Cambodia are not quite as big as those in Takeo Province, but when they're done with you, you look like you have a bad case of chickenpox!

There are more people now than before, though no one waves or even looks at you. At the same time, they all look like they've seen a ghost or something. And I soon understand why.

We are stopped by the Khmer Rouge. There's no doubt this is who it is. As always, the black pajamas and red-checkered scarves they wear as angrily as they do proudly give them away.

They literally pull us off the bike.

"Come with us!" one of them says.

Père says nothing. He is only trying to protect us because every Cambodian now knows nothing good comes from making these angry rebels even madder.

They walk us off the path and into the thick of the jungle. We know what this means. *Everyone knows what this means.* If they select you for the *short walk,* you're as good as dead.

When we get into the woods, we notice there are dead bodies everywhere. This is the odor I caught earlier. The stench of human flesh rotting is unlike any other smell. You know exactly what it is when you smell it. And once that smell is stamped on your brain, you never forget it.

I start to close my eyes, but right before I do, I see Père kneeling and begging, almost even praying his plea I would say. *"Please let us go. I have nothing to give you. Please let us go."*

I am pushed to the ground. I just sit there… and close my eyes. I know what's about to happen. I hear my père – my *father* – as he continues to beg and pray, beg and pray. This seems to go on forever. I'm waiting for the shots. I'm waiting just to be done with everything – the hunger, the thirst, the exhaustion, the confusion… and the smell.

I accept all of this, all that is about to happen. It's not that I'm courageous or bold, not by a long shot. I'm just over it all. I accept what is happening because I have nothing more to resist with. I have no strength, no will, no emotion even. At this point I just don't care.

So I just close my eyes and wait. *Let's get it done.*

I can hear father continuing to beg, somewhere over to the left. I hear him begging, *"please, please, please, please, please!"*

The next thing I know, we're back on the bicycle again! I have no idea why or how or what actually happened. I just know we are spared. Somehow.

At first, we just chug along. Père does not want to give the impression that we are trying to hurriedly flee. That simple act could be enough to cause a soldier to change his mind and shoot us in the back. A bit down the trail Père stops without warning. Maybe he stops to gather himself after being seconds away from a capricious death. He doesn't say. And he wouldn't want to frighten me… his little boy.

But I'm glad we stop. There's a man on the side of the road and he has a big water jug, the kind with the spigot at the bottom. He's selling water.

I don't do a lot of running these days, but I run now – and with all the speed I can muster. Even before I get there, I can taste the water. I can feel it soothing the fire in my throat and washing away the dust in my mouth. Without even thinking, I run to the man with the jug, pull it from him, turn the spout and drink.

Once again, I hear Père begging. *"Please, I don't have any money to give you, please forgive us. We don't have any money; we don't have anything for you. I know he's thirsty, please, please…."*

I am ashamed to say that I don't even know if Père got any water.

And then we're back on the bicycle.

I am completely disheartened to find that – after all we've been through already on this journey – the next section is the most treacherous. It is through the most heavily guarded area of the entire trip. The Khmer Rouge know where the refugee camps are. They know that's where everybody wants to go. And they intend to either profit from it or see to it that you don't make it.

It's not hard to understand what's going on here. The Khmer Rouge know you're trying to get to freedom, and they know the road you have to take to do that. So they wait for you there, to take everything from you. And they usually kill you if you don't have anything to give them.

Imagine you're a fisherman. There's a stream of salmon. You know where the salmon go to spawn. You know which way they're headed, so you simply go there and wait to catch them. That's exactly what the Khmer Rouge are doing with us.

We can only do one thing now, and that is to *run the gauntlet*. This is no game. It is a real life-and-death situation.

Even though I saw it firsthand, even though I experienced it many times, it's hard even now to imagine that kind of callousness – that kind of *pure hatred*. If they can't profit from you, then they will take pleasure in killing your hope… killing *you*. That's just how it works. Why they let us go I can only assign to Providence.

The gauntlet stretches from the road we're on to the refugee camp. And there are many obstacles in between as I later learn, including the long road through the jungle and then through the rice paddy. After the rice paddy there's a wide river to cross, and then a field, and then finally the refugee camp.

And at any time, without any warning, you can be shot.

Because of the nature of everything that's going on, the refugee camp is heavily guarded by the Thai army. So it's not just about crossing the border. You actually aren't safe until you reach the camp, a few hundred yards *inside* the border.

Besides, the Thai guards don't just let you come in. They aren't waiting for you with open arms, ready to welcome you into their country. In fact, you can get killed there just as easily.

It's almost too fantastic to believe. To make it safely inside the Thai camp this is what you're up against: You have to first survive the Khmer Rouge, as well as the natural obstacles on land and in water along the trail. Then there's the Thai army that may shoot at you if you try to come into their country, because they don't know if you're friend or foe. And, if that's not enough, the anti-communist counterinsurgency randomly shoot at the Khmer Rouge every chance they get. So you're just as likely to get caught in their crossfire as not.

We reach a point where we can no longer continue on the road because there are just so many people. We don't know where to go next, but there are people who do know. Père finds somebody who can help us, so we join this group of escapees trying to get to the Thai refugee camp. I have no idea who Père has to pay – or if he has anything to pay with. But we are *in*.

There are maybe 15 people in our group, including some young kids. One woman has a baby, another has a small toddler who's maybe two. Even though I'm only six myself, I'm amazed at how helpless a baby is, and how senseless it is that a baby and a little boy have to be here. What a horrible thing… to put people in a circumstance where a mother has to protect her baby by exposing it to this awful place and situation. And my next thought is that I'm not much better off. I have to somehow survive this too.

Before long Père says "Get up on my back." I instantly obey. And he puts some kind of sling around me for support that also goes over his shoulders.

We're back in the jungle. For how long I don't know. We again hear those frightening animal sounds that I've come to hate. But like everybody else I understand that this is just part of it.

That's not the only sound echoing through the jungle, however. There's the crack of a gunshot. And then another. And then out of nowhere everybody starts running, including Père – and me, held on by that sling. Turns out we're being chased… and shot at… by the Khmer Rouge.

We're running like mad, with this group of kids and adults trying to escape to Thailand. We run out of the jungle and through rice fields, and we still hear guns. There's a stand of bushes in sight, so everybody heads for the bushes. Thorns and branches tear at and scrape my face, legs, and arms. I imagine what they must be doing to Père because he is in front.

The bushes we're in are in water, which means so are we. The water's cold and covered with mosquitoes.

And there are those smells again. Offsetting the clean smell of the sweet grass is that dreadfully awful odor of death, the stagnant water and whatever's in it, and all the sweating bodies. It's a crazy mix of fragrance and odor playing with your nose and your mind.

Nobody complains, though. I'm sure the adults are scared out of their wits however, just trying to get themselves and us kids out of here alive. I just want this to be over. I'm so tired. So hungry. If I knew how to pray, I'd be praying for this madness to end.

"Don't move!" Père whispers sharply, in response to my restless attention to all my scratches and cuts. Besides, I'm sure there are snakes in this water, too. It's Cambodia, after all. There has to be. I just make myself be still and try not to make a sound.

Hours pass. Then people slowly start stirring and getting up, which suits me just fine. I don't feel like walking, but it beats lying in the wet bushes. So we start again. The Khmer Rouge must be far enough away now, but they won't be forever. So we move.

We stay close together. Until we hear more gunshots… and then everybody scatters and runs back to the bushes. Again. Hours later, we risk moving again only to hear gunshots a third time. It isn't until we do this routine for a few times over that we are finally able to move on.

After walking a bit farther, we get lucky. We have to go through some tall grass – taller than me when I'm standing up. Tall and thick. And it feels safe, sort of… I'm just glad we're finally out of the swamp and bushes.

We seem to stay in the grass for hours.

Slowly but surely night comes. Along with it are the crickets and all the other night-loving insects. I think to myself that they sing beautifully together – as if they all belong to some strange choir.

It doesn't make sense. All around us people are shooting and bombing and killing. We could die any minute. And we know it.

But when I look up, I see a bird flying overhead. Just flying. Free. *Why can't we be like that?* Up there is peace and beauty.

12

Out of the Darkness

It's important to remember that this story is running in several veins concurrently. While Père and I are on our strange journey that begins with the long bicycle ride covered in chapter 11, other members of my family are facing their own struggles.

Sidan gives us the account of what he and those with him are facing:

Life at Camp Seven is like being caught in some kind of holding pattern. All we can do is sit, wait, and watch… for Sideth. I feel so useless and restless, like I should be doing something to help see to it that he gets here safely.

Sovannary and I have no way of knowing if our little brother is even still alive… and if he is, how the trip is going. We have no idea who signed up for the harrowing mission of bringing him to us, and we certainly don't know if it's working.

One fact we are both keenly aware of is just how dangerous this journey is, and how many people *don't* make it. Sadly, we also know that it is just as likely he and his courier *won't* make it either. Because we can't bear to go there, we say nothing about it at all.

It's March now, which is our dry season. Hot and dry. But regardless of the weather, it's a very dangerous trip to this camp.

While sitting alone outside the hut lost in my thoughts, I notice a small circle of dust in the distance getting larger, and closer. For all the world it looks as if it's heading in our direction.

The closer it gets, the more I can tell it is a person, or maybe a group of people; I can't be sure. Or maybe it's Aunt Sim coming back. I'm really straining now to see, and before long I can tell that it *is* Aunt Sim! I call my sister and she comes running out of the hut.

True to form, Aunt Sim is bearing gifts of food and money and gold – though no one in the camp can know about the money and the gold – for our safety as well as the advantage it gives us when we might need it most.

We eat and talk and catch up. In the middle of our visit I notice a sense of peace come over me that I haven't felt in a long time. I think it's because at that moment I believe in my heart that we're really trying – and that there might really be a chance, however slight, that we will see Sideth again. At least Aunt Sim's presence reminds me how hard we're trying.

"It's been four days since Ny Keo's contact left to go get Sideth," our aunt says.

My only response is, "yes."

She looks at me. "How long did you say it took you to get here?"

"About a day and a half," I tell her, "not counting the time we spent in Nam
Chong."

Nam Chong is the holding place where we stayed a few days, but you can actually go right through it if you are so inclined, provided there is no fighting going on at the time.

And of course, we know the length of the journey all depends on what happens in between – what kind of trouble you run into. Then there's the situation as you get nearer to Camp Seven of whether or not the Khmer Rouge are patrolling heavily. This makes it harder... and longer, to get through.

Aunt Sim says, "Okay." She looks straight ahead. "Okay," she repeats. "There are a lot of variables. We know that. But they could be here tonight. Or it could be tomorrow night. They should be coming out of that field over there, to the southeast." She indicates the direction. We all look. "That's if everything goes according to plan."

I wonder if the route they're taking right now is easier than mine was. I sure hope so. And I certainly hope that Sideth's arriving safely doesn't involve him having to breathe under water through a reed. I just can't see the little guy succeeding at that at his age.

Sovannary's silence through all this is speaking volumes.

Every so often Ny Keo comes by and sits next to Sovannary, or she gets up and stands next to him. They say things to each other that I can't hear and frankly don't care to know. Somewhere in the conversation he always manages to rub her stomach.

As we sit and wait, another hot day turns to dusk and the sun hurries toward the horizon. Night is when the anxiety really kicks into high gear. Already you can hear the whine of an AK47 screaming beyond the thick jungle.

Another night, another soul stolen. Every time I hear a *CRACK!* it feels a little like it's blowing a hole through my own gut. Please God, don't let it be my little brother.

So here we sit – Aunt Sim, Sovannary, and me. We all sit in this same spot most all the time. And at least one of us is always awake and watching.

Because the two stories are so interconnected at this juncture, I want to tell what's going with Père and me at this very same time.

It seems like only minutes ago that I was watching the stars and dreaming about how it would feel to be free like the birds that fly randomly across the evening sky. But I must have fallen asleep, because the next thing I know it's day. And the sky above now is the prettiest blue I've ever seen.

Our little group of people are still hiding in the tall grass. A welcome breeze wanders past every now and again. All the trees and proud blades of grass move in unison, cooling my sweaty body and causing me to be grateful.

When the breeze stops, we all get up and get moving again. And when you hear gunshots you go low into the grass, or bushes, or whatever you have near to hide in.

I remember once having nothing but the bare ground to fall on. I lay there imagining myself able to disappear under the dirt so I can't be seen… or hit by a bullet. The shooting stops and once again we start moving forward in fits and starts, trying desperately to get to wherever we are going to get away from here.

Most of the time I walk, at least when I can. But when we really must move quickly, Père puts me on his back again. "You're a good boy," he tells me. And his words feel like a gift.

When we are able to move slowly, I feel safe to look around, and I notice how beautiful my country is. At least here, at least this part, is as beautiful as a dream. The sun highlights every blade of grass and every leaf of every tree. The lush green rice paddies and rich green mountains sitting here and there, the palm trees and waves of tall grass all around, all look like a beautiful painting. In fact, it's so serene and I'm so tired and weak that when I'm on Père's back, I doze off from time to time.

As I sleep, or maybe I am awake – I can hardly tell the difference – I see rays of sun breaking through a cloud, like angels opening a doorway to heaven. I imagine that the angels come through that doorway and pick up those of us who are traveling. Maybe that's where we're headed. Maybe we're all on our way to heaven. Maybe we're just one bedraggled, earth-weary group of pilgrims being taken to a much, much better place.

Wherever we are going, no one is talking. Even as we walk through the grass following our guide – the guy that everyone is trusting with their life to keep us safe and lead us to the right place – no one in our group makes a sound. Only the guide speaks now and then, to someone toward the front. Of course, I have no idea what he's saying.

But then my thoughts are interrupted by the sight of something I was not expecting – a river. A wide river. And a wooden fishing boat about 25 feet long is tied up by the bank. There are no paddles. Instead, one person stands at the back of the boat with a long wooden stick that he uses to push off from the bottom of the river and get the boat in motion.

I don't know what kind of logistics are worked out, or what kinds of decisions are made. But the next thing I know, we're all being rushed into the boat. Père and I get on, along with everyone else in our party, with not an inch to spare between us. Somebody pushes the boat off. We head out into the water with a boat full of way more people than it was meant to carry. (It was built to hold 10 people.)

Once we're well away from the shore, I realize how easily this small wooden boat could flip over. We're practically sitting on top of each other. But at least for now, we're still upright. And we're still moving, however slowly. This river is so wide though, that you can't see the other side from where we are. It just seems to go on and on.

Someone shifts, and we almost flip. It happens again, but miraculously the boat is righted, and we keep moving. One mass of people all piled on top of one another and moving slowly, so slowly, down the river for what seems like an hour. And we're still not there.

Maybe it's a lake, not a river. I don't know. What I do know is that I just want us to get to the other side. I keep looking… looking… and finally, after what feels like an eternity, I can see land again. Thank goodness, the shore is in sight.

Père and I have gone from the bike on the road to traveling with this group of refugees on foot through the jungle and tall grasses of the rice paddy, to riding the boat across the water, and now to the other side. And we made it. We made it through all that. Not only that, I can now barely see huts across the field, looking like little matchboxes placed here and there at will.

We're staring across a clearing, a field of grass, and beyond that is the camp. It's about half a kilometer (over a quarter mile) away, but you can still see it.

It comes as no surprise, but this clearing is watched – or more correctly, *guarded*. Somehow I know that, even before the guide who brought us here whispers it. He tells us to be very quiet. I notice the woman covering her baby's mouth. For a brief second, I wonder whether they can make it across the field without getting shot.

It's time to cross the field, so we all start running. There's a gunshot… and then another. One of our companions is struck down. We duck into the tall grass and stay there, and stay *down*, until everything is quiet again. Then we repeat the process. We run like our life depends on it (it does)… then wait. Run… then wait. Run… wait. Bullets are whizzing all around us.

I'm terrified. Surely I'm not the only one. But we have to keep moving. *Everything* you have goes into that. You can't stop and think about being scared half to death, even if you are. You have to keep moving forward. We do, but it feels like we're in that field forever.

We don't know it, but we are now very near Sidan, Sovannary, and Aunt Sim. Sidan picks up the story from their point of view:

Maybe this will be the day... or rather, the night. I keep saying that, but it's all the hope we have. At any rate, this *should* be. If there is a reason for it not to be, I don't want to think about it.

We sit in our usual spot near the front of Camp Seven – Sovannary, Aunt Sim, and I. There is no gate or entrance, *per se,* to Camp Seven. It's just where everything *starts,* if you know what I mean.

We talk only about what matters. And even then, we keep our conversation short and sweet, like "This has to be the night. And if it isn't, then tomorrow, for sure. But this has to be it."

Time crawls. We sit in silence now. The sun is low. I can see the reflection of the red evening sun on Aunt Sim's face. She looks worried. I get that. The deadline is real. The stakes couldn't be higher. It's as if the universe is hanging on what happens tonight. In fact, *our universe is!*

For some reason, we all feel like tonight is the night we will know.

Aunt Sim is troubled. She doesn't want to show it – the last thing she wants to do is add to Sovannary and Sidan's already bulging concerns. She adds the following to fill in Sidan's narrative above:

As we sit here in worried silence, my mind travels to my own immediate family across the border. At this very moment it's possible that they have already left for the Thai camp where they will be readied for sponsorship to the States. I know this is quite possible. And that thought wrenches my heart.

But Sovannary, and Sidan... and little Sideth out there... God knows, they are my family too. No, my *children* too.

But if I'm perfectly honest, I'm torn in half. I *hate* having to choose between them and the rest of my family right now. But I'm in the right place. I *know* I am.

Sometimes life presents you with a situation where you have to choose – and there is no good option because the situation itself is so horrible. But once you decide, and the moment of reckoning is at your door, you know you chose well because, in the middle of the turmoil, you're almost at peace. I can almost even smile about being here right now. Almost.

It's now 3:00 a.m. and we're all wide awake.

All of a sudden, we run with all our might – straight through this field, straight across the middle. Everyone just runs for dear life, except for those little ones being carried. I'm on Père's back the whole time. Thank God for my Père!

Once again, bullets are coming from every direction. We keep running. Tragically, I see people around me dropping from gunfire. I hope they're wounded and not dead. *We are so close.*

We run… we just keep running. I'm still on Père's back and we're still running. That's all I know.

From Sidan's end, it all looks like this:

> How quickly a situation can change. In the glow of the moonlight a group of gray silhouettes appear out of the tall grass and seem to be running across the field between us.
>
> Aunt Sim nudges me, even though I already see it. I hear her gasp, *"Holy God!"*
>
> We're all wide awake now, to say the least.
>
> Sovannary makes some kind of sound, a little scream of excitement – or horror, as if it just inadvertently leaked out of her mouth.
>
> Now I know that we all see it; it's not my eyes playing with me, or my mind and heart creating what I want to see. In the light of the moon we all see this group of shapes, running across the field… and they are headed straight toward the camp!
>
> We sit helpless. Hopeful… but helpless! All we can do is stare and pray. Stare and pray as they run across no-man's-land. Many, many have been dropped there before. A special cruelty.
>
> Tracer bullets seem like shooting stars in the night. Only here they are horizontal – and just above ground level. We are keenly aware that at any moment any bullet can connect with any person.
>
> And that would end their all-out pursuit for freedom. Just like that. Over and done with, just when the prize is in sight. But I can't allow myself to think about that now. Not now.
>
> A few minutes more and we can now see them, as people. *Specific* people.
>
> "It's *him!*"
>
> I think we all said it at once as *one triumphal shout of praise.*
>
> Seeing my little brother on Père's back… I recognize him, and then them. *It is them alright!*
>
> Père falls.

Sideth falls with him, of course, like some big doll strapped to his back.

Collectively, we hold our breath.

He's moving again, thank God! *Père is moving!* He gets up again and starts running... and all the while they are getting visibly clearer, closer, bigger. But it is taking forever.

A tracer bullet flies past, just missing them. And then another. Some evil fool hoping to get lucky, hoping their bullet is the one that hits somebody, so they can brag for five minutes to their sick comrades.

I curse them to the ends of the Earth. Then say a quick, but maybe the most heartfelt prayer I've ever prayed, for these dear people to make it. These who are giving their all to make it to freedom.

13

When Barely is Enough

My foster father is still running – carrying me in the sling – through this field in the dead of night. Tracers from AK47s are everywhere, flying about in all directions. We're getting shot at from soldiers in front of us... and from the Khmer Rouge behind us! I don't know why soldiers up ahead are shooting at us – or why we keep running *toward* them – but we do!

I later find out that the soldiers in front of us were not shooting at us but at whoever's trying to kill us from behind. That's why they're not hitting us. But at the time I don't understand any of it. I don't know what is happening.

I just know I'm tied to Père. And I'm glad, because there is no way I could hold onto him, and I surely couldn't run on my own. I have no energy left. Once again, I am in that familiar place where I don't even have enough energy to be afraid.

I can't believe Père has the strength to keep running. In fact, he tripped once already, and we fell hard. But then he got up and took off again.

How is he doing this? How is he strong enough to carry me and keep running for our lives through this field? I can't imagine...

Then the next thing I know the shooting stops. And I see people ahead of us cheering, and some are crying. We made it to the camp. *We actually made it!*

And that's the last thing I remember.

From my family inside the camp it looks like this:

"They're here! They're safe! They made it... Père and Sideth are here!" says Sidan. As soon as they get inside camp territory, Père collapses, still holding Sideth – brave, wonderful, loving Père!

We run over to them. When I get close enough to see him, my heart stops and I can't breathe. It looks like Sideth is dead. He's lifeless, limp. He's not moving at all in Père's arms.

"He's... alive." Père can barely whisper he's so weak and tired himself. "Needs water..."

I throw myself on Père with the biggest, most sincere hug I've ever given. I try to hug Sideth but he is so weak. Little, near lifeless Sideth. My baby brother is here. Aunt Sim and Sovannary run to bring them food and water.

People throughout the camp are sharing food and water with the new arrivals. Some of them can barely move, barely eat.

Sideth's mouth is open and some water is going in with the help of Aunt Sim. Sovannary is right there too, assisting. They're doing all they can to take care of him. They're holding him... hugging him. He hasn't said anything yet.

He's so swollen from starvation – worse than I've ever seen. Besides how terribly big his stomach is, his ankles are twice as wide as his legs. They look like they're too wide for him to walk. It breaks my heart.

And he still hasn't moved. Or said anything. Or even voluntarily opened his mouth.

But he's here. And if, God forbid, he dies, he will die with us.

Aunt Sim hugs him again, then Sovannary, then me. Then Aunt Sim hugs Père, who thankfully is able to eat and drink a little. In fact, we all take turns hugging him.

I notice Sideth moving his mouth like he's trying to say something, but nothing comes out.

Then something happens we aren't expecting. I don't know who starts it, but as soon as one of us does, we all do. We all just start bawling.

We are crying because of the condition Sideth is in and for everything he's gone through – for everything we've all gone through. It's so pitiful.

We're crying because of the sacrifice and risk that Père took to bring Sideth to us. We're crying because all that's left of our nuclear family – the three of us – are miraculously still alive, still here.

It's a lot of awful stuff. But it's also the opposite. It's like when you can't put what you're feeling into words because it's all too much. It's all too big and too emotional.

Aunt Sim says something encouraging, and Sovannary nods. I don't know what she said, but I'm glad to see Sovannary nod. For some strange reason, that feels good to me.

To Père, who loved so much and sacrificed so much for us all, we hand over everything we have – all the gold and silver and money, as well as any extra food for his trip back. *And all, every last drop, of our full and collective gratitude.*

Then we sit with him and talk for a while and share our stories. We talk about everything they had to go through to get here. The whole time we talk, Aunt Sim and Sovannary hold and rock Sideth.

And thankfully he's starting to come around; he's trying to talk. That's good. We'll take anything.

Somehow, without even knowing it's coming, I drop off to sleep.

It's daylight when I wake up. I'm surprised to learn that Père is nowhere to be found. He's already gone. How he found the strength to leave so soon I'll never know.

I also learn on waking that Aunt Sim and Sovannary were up all night with Sideth. Aunt Sim says, "We have to get him to Khao-I-Dang as soon as possible. They have medicine there, and hopefully the UN and Red Cross can help." Aunt Sim always knows what to do.

As it turns out, there were other reasons we needed to get to Khao-I-Dang right away. Time was very tight as far as the departure deadline is concerned. In fact, I had no idea just how tight.

14

A Difference of Two Days

I don't remember anything after the night run through the field dodging bullets, until I wake up in the refugee camp in Cambodia.

I did learn later that as soon as Père returned me safely to my family, he left to go back to his wife and other children. He knows he is needed there. This all happened over a few hours. Of course, I wasn't aware of any of it; I was intermittently either unconscious or delirious.

I hate one thing about all of this, and it is so sad to me. After that night I never saw Père again. The man that risked his life for me – a child that just showed up at his doorstep one day. A child he had only known for about a year.

Why did he do it? He was promised money, of course. Money and jewelry, which my aunt gave him. Hopefully that all made a difference and allowed him to buy enough food for his family to survive the famine. I can only hope… and pray… that he made it safely back home to find them all still alive.

But I'll never believe he did it just for the money he was promised. That level of sacrifice, that kind of risk, is rooted in nothing less than pure love. No husband and wife take in a pitiful band of disparate orphans – when they barely have enough to feed themselves and their own children – out of anything but pure love!

Christ said the highest form of love is when someone gives their life for another. That's what Père risked for me. And not just for what he put himself through to return me to my family. He also saved my life every day I lived with him and Mère. Every day. They are heroes – plain and simple.

As you remember, our family story is also playing out on another front. Listen to these words from my cousin Malis:

> Days pass… and my father and I have no idea what's happening with my mother and Sovannary and Sidan… and whether Sideth…
>
> We're in Khao-I-Dang, going about our business, doing our jobs, awaiting the inevitable. Though I know our deadline must be approaching, I don't bring it up. Father doesn't either. One thing we do know is this. Mother hasn't forgotten us, and she is doing everything she can for our family – *all* of our family.
>
> We're trying to keep busy, all the while not knowing when we'll be called to leave. When it's time, you know you'll be torn in two. You're torn now even, worrying about what might happen if your family is separated.
>
> What will my father do, I wonder, if they say it's time to go? Will I go with him or stay and wait for Mother and my cousins? I don't think either of us really knows what we'll do if that possibility becomes our reality.

After months apart, all that is left of my immediate family – Sovannary, Sidan, and myself – are finally, *miraculously* together again.

But there's still a major problem facing us. We're on the wrong side of the border!

Sidan explains:

> It isn't safe in the camps in Cambodia. The Thai camp is where we must be. Our ultimate goal is to get to America. In order to do that, you have to have your name on the refugee list and then you have to be selected for sponsorship. And all that happens in Thailand.
>
> But we are facing a bigger problem. The Americans have stopped taking people from the camp in Cambodia to the camp in Thailand. Their military trucks aren't transporting people anymore. I don't know if it is a policy change or what. At any rate, these trips have stopped.
>
> Not only that, the Thai camp is heavily guarded… from the Khmer Rouge as well as the people fighting the Khmer Rouge.

So, the only way to get it done is to pay someone to guide you to the Thai camp. And as with every other journey here, it is a perilous undertaking. And you have to travel at night.

There is a group of us, a good 40 people counting Aunt Sim, Sideth and me. Sovannary stays behind. This is the last thing the rest of us want. But we understand. She is married now and beyond that, she and my brother-in-law are anticipating their first child. It's perfectly reasonable she stays… but it hurts deeply to leave her behind.

Aunt Sim has this whole thing planned out for us. We pack up our stuff, which isn't much, say our goodbyes to Sovannary and Ny Keo. And we leave.

Our route through the woods in the dark goes on for a long time. I have Sideth on my back in a sling Aunt Sim made. He is far too weak to walk. It is maybe a mile on foot, from one camp to the other. We all move as quietly as possible so as not to alert our enemies.

We finally get through the woods and to an area with a barbed wire fence. There is a guard tower right above us. It seems we are here for an alarming amount of time, but then time always seems to crawl in these circumstances. I have no idea how long we actually wait.

Finally, there is a flash from a light overhead. It's a signal from the guard up in the tower. I later learn that it is in response to a signal from our well-paid guide on the ground. The guide you pay must know the guard too – and share the pay with him. If you are there without a guide that has connections, you will be shot. That's how this game works.

They don't roll out the red carpet, or even open the gate; they simply don't shoot at us. And that is enough. Our guide pulls up the barbed wire, and one by one we crawl under it. Another event which seems to take forever.

Aunt Sim is amazing. She has saved our lives – *again*. You have to know what you are doing to get across the border. You have to know how to play the game it requires. And you have to have money. Thankfully, we have Aunt Sim… and she has the money and the know-how.

Finally… gratefully, we are in Thailand. It has been a journey fraught with all sorts of unimaginables. It has been a journey that, for much of the way, Sidan and I have taken alone, in the sense of being apart from one another and from Sovannary.

We are in the same country now as Aunt Sim's family, but she, Sidan, and I are still not *with* them. My cousin, Malis, shares with us what life is like for Uncle Kari and her at the time of our arrival in Thailand (my other cousins are there of course, but are too young to be involved to any degree).

Remember, they are well into the two-week deadline for their departure, and the pressure is mounting.

Malis says:

Father and I continue going through the motions, taking care of the younger children, and hoping with everything in us that the rest of our family gets here before we have to leave.

Then, one morning I wake to find that my mom, Sidan, and Sideth are here! That is such good... no, *great* news!

But of course, these days seem to guarantee that what good news there is never comes unaccompanied. There is always bad news lurking. And this time, the bad news is that Sideth is very, very sick.

The other piece of sad news is that Sovannary is not with them. Naturally, she stayed back with her husband. Sovannary and I are very close, so that broke my heart. But I understand. She married a soldier who has a job to do in the Cambodian camp. And she is pregnant with his child.

Looking back on everything that happened, I believe that if Sovannary had not left our family and returned to the refugee camp in Cambodia, we would never have reconnected with Sidan and Sideth. Without that return trip, her subsequent marriage would not have occurred.

And then the reason Sidan came to the border was because he heard about Sovannary's marriage into a family of means. Had she not returned to Camp Seven, that would not have happened. And once Sovannary and Sidan found each other again, they were able – with Mother's help – to put a plan together to bring Sideth to the border as well.

Then while Mother, Sovannary, and Sidan are working to find a way to bring Sideth to the border, my Father receives news that our family has been chosen for sponsorship to America. Father sends word to Mother who is now at the camp. And Mother decides she is not leaving without Sideth.

Providentially it all worked out, though. Sideth arrives with his foster father just in time for Mother, Sidan and Sideth to get back to Khao-I-Dang. Now, we can all leave for America together, as one family.

Everything is a blur for me when Père and I arrive at the Cambodian camp because by then, I am so malnourished and close to death that I don't know what world I'm in. Another reason is because no sooner did we arrive at Camp Seven than we are on the move again, this time to Khao-I-Dang in Thailand.

By the time we get to Khao-I-Dang the ball is already in motion for everyone to leave there for Chon Buri. So we're only in Khao-I-Dang for two days before leaving for the camp at Chon Buri. Gratefully, this latter camp is run by Americans.

Another wonder is in play as well. When Uncle Kari gets my name on the list, we're not even at Khao-I-Dang yet! He had no idea where we were. In faith and desperate hope, he just asked that my name be added.

Just *two days* made all the difference in our life – our future. We make it to Khao-I-Dang just in time for Sidan and me to be included. And just in time for Aunt Sim to rejoin her family so they don't have to leave without her – or have to face the horrible decision of whether to leave at all.

But we make it. We are here. We are all here and we're ready to leave together… as one *family*.

Our Refugee Family. Back Row l-r: Uncle Kari and Aunt Sim,
cousins Alynn (in arms), Malis, Moldavy, Meanrith, Annette.
Front Row l-r: Morokath, Meta, my brother Sidan, and me (Sideth).

15

The Wait is Over

Just two days after arriving at Khao-I-Dang we all get on the bus and go to Chon Buri – a transition camp for refugees in Thailand that is run by the United Nations. (That's what the "CB" in the front of the number my uncle is holding up in our family portrait stands for.)

The first checkpoint in Chon Buri is a health screening to make sure we don't have any health issues that would prevent us from going to America. Just getting a checkup is nerve-racking, because it could mean some of us will have to remain behind. Aunt Kim and Uncle Kari were especially worried that I would not pass the brief physical. Thankfully, we all check out okay.

While here, we learn how to use running water and the toilet. We are also taught some English and some of the American ways. But one of the best things about Chon Buri is that we have regular meals. Living conditions are much better and more civilized here than what we had in Cambodia.

We also get vaccinated here, and I get cleaned up. In fact, Malis scrubs me so hard it hurts!

We pass all the initial requirements – but then nothing happens. Although we are ready for departure, we don't yet have a sponsor. It is impossible to leave the country without that critical component in place. And there are hundreds of people just like us at Chon Buri – which is but one of several staging camps – all waiting for sponsorship. So more than anything, we learn to be patient.

Months pass, and we are still waiting. In fact, we're at Chon Buri for a total of six months.

And then somehow, with so very many of us still waiting for sponsorship, a missionary and his wife – Jerry and Libby Percifield, who are connected with the Catholic Foundation, sign up to sponsor our family of 11.

It all started when a member of Libby's family shared all the refugee problems going on in Thailand with Jerry and Libby. Because they wanted to find out how they could help, Jerry and Libby signed up with the Catholic Relief Services organization.

About a month later they visited one of the refugee camps. While waiting for their plane to take them back to the U.S., Jerry got a call from the Catholic Foundation. "Hey, we got a family of nine that you need to sponsor. It's very important."

Those nine people were my uncle and aunt and their seven children. Sidan and I were not on the list at that point. But somehow, some way, my uncle was able to get Sidan and me added to the list once he found out. (I believe my aunt had to sell her wedding ring to make it happen.) They sent a picture of all 11 of us to Jerry and his wife. And they said, *"Yes, we'll sponsor them all."*

I don't know why they called Jerry, though. And I don't know what made them choose my aunt and uncle... because there were so many people waiting to be sponsored in that one refugee camp alone.

But once my uncle got the green light that someone or some organization was going to sponsor us, we were ready to get on a plane for Bataan in the Philippines... the next stop on our journey to America.

The Philippines

Bataan, another military-based refugee holding camp, is our new temporary home. This camp is different though, as there are Laotians and Vietnamese here, in addition to Cambodians. A group of Buddhist monks that had been persecuted by the Khmer Rouge are also here.

Most of the Cambodian refugees will likely end up in America. Since we helped America fight the Vietnamese from 1970-1975, America feels a certain loyalty to Cambodia. Canada and Australia also agree to accept refugees into their countries as well.

Bataan is where all the paperwork is completed. You have to wait your turn to get your paperwork done. That's okay though… we have a sponsor! Even then, there is a certain suspense hanging over our heads. What if our sponsors change their minds once they find out they have to come to Bataan?

Jerry and Libby agreed to sponsor us when we were still in Khao-I-Dang. But in order to complete the process and make it official, they have to come to Bataan *in person* to finish the paperwork. Everything has to work, everything has to be done and in order, before you can leave for the States.

The military base managing the refugees in Bataan is well organized. For instance, while we are here, we attend school. We also go to church, or should I say church comes to us. We all meet up in a large pavilion for services.

We are fed regular meals and given vaccinations. On Fridays, someone from the church or the base brings a movie, along with popcorn and candy for us all. This is my favorite part of our orientation to America!

We get to watch *The Ten Commandments* with Charlton Heston and *Superman* with Christopher Reeve and Margot Kidder. We also see one movie about a Beetle car that drives itself. And to top it off, along with our popcorn and candy we get Coca-Cola… with ice!

But the best thing about Bataan to me is that I am neither malnourished nor even hungry anymore. Even still, my family continues calling me *Haem* ("swollen"). You might recall this was the nickname given me by someone in one of the Cambodian camps. It is a reference back to my starving days, when I had the telltale distended abdomen.

Here there is plenty rice and chicken and fish. The United Nations provide most of what we eat from somewhere in the Philippines. The Philippines share similar cultures and cuisines with Cambodia. This means the food here is very familiar to us.

Before long I get my energy back, which means I can join in with other refugee kids. This is the first time in my life that I get to do things most kids do every day. And I am really happy here… until I think about my family. Nobody explains anything to me about what is going on, so I do a lot of wondering. I wonder where the rest of my family are, and if I will ever be with them again.

Sidan is a full eight years older than me. For whatever reason he isn't around much now. Instead, my cousin Malis takes care of me. She bathes me, sees that I have food, and makes sure I am happy.

According to the paperwork completed in Bataan, I am now seven years old. It's early 1981, and I was born in February 1972. But because I have been so malnourished all my life, I look more like a five-year-old than a nine-year-old. At the same time, to set my age at five would make me four years younger than I actually am. So, I can only assume that's why the authorities put my age at seven, to help as best they could for when I start school.

After being in Bataan close to six months, we get word that everything is finally ready for us to leave for America. By now, it is spring of 1981.

Between 1975 and 1994, America allowed 149,000 refugees and 6,000 immigrants into the country. (The difference between a refugee and an immigrant is that a refugee is someone seeking refuge in another country because they are fleeing their own country. An immigrant is someone who chooses, without duress, to resettle in another country.)

In time, most of the refugees settled in parts of California – Long Beach, Fresno and Stockton… Cleveland, Ohio… Providence, Rhode Island… a couple cities in Massachusetts… Seattle, Washington… Portland, Oregon… and other parts of the Pacific Northwest.

Providence leads us elsewhere. For us, our landing spot is in Georgia.

PART 3

16

America At Last!

It is April 1981. We all board a plane in the Philippines on our way to Atlanta, Georgia. As the weather would have it, we fly through a lot of turbulence on that 17-hour journey. Most everyone gets sick. Everyone but me, that is. It turns out that I actually love flying! And for some reason the turbulence doesn't bother me.

They give us peanuts and later even serve us a full meal. But the most interesting treat we get is this cheese wrapped in wax that is like paper. It has a picture of a cow on the label and is called *Laughing Cow*. To my young mind this is such a funny thing – a laughing cow! That cheese is the best thing I ever had. I unwrap my surprise, pop it in my mouth, and at that moment believe I am the happiest little boy in all the world.

After what seems like forever, we land at Hartsfield Airport in Atlanta. The building is *huge*, and clean, and there are so many people coming and going and walking everywhere. Everyone looks very nice and clean… and as I look around, I think to myself, *"I'm going to be like them one day."*

Jerry picks us up at the airport in a station wagon. It is night and sitting in the back I can see all the lights of the city. I can't believe all the lights and how beautiful they are. And everything is so peaceful (or maybe I'm just sleepy). Nobody talks, because we're all exhausted from the flight, not to mention all that we have gone through to get to this point.

I must have fallen asleep while counting streetlights because the next thing I know we're at Jerry and Libby's house.

No one could ever doubt that these good people truly care about our wellbeing. They make sure we have clothes and shoes. One of the first things Libby does is trace around our feet as each of us stands on a sheet of paper. She is getting our shoe sizes so they can buy us all shoes that fit. They feed us well. They do everything they can to help us adapt to American life as easily and quickly as possible.

We're learning a lot more English now – from listening to other people, like Jerry and Libby and their daughter, and from people on TV and in the movies. One of the best ways we learn is by asking questions.

We stay with Jerry and Libby for two or three months, while they help us find a more permanent place to live. Their home is large, but with 11 extra people, it is more than a full house! The kids sleep on the floor. Libby makes a pallet out of blankets for Sidan and me, and we sleep on the floor in the garage.

They have a daughter that my cousins and I play with, or should I say the others play with, all the time. I am more interested in the beautiful garden Libby has growing in the backyard. It is full of berries of all kinds… and loads of vegetables. I love everything in the garden, but especially the black and red berries.

A beautiful park with lots of blooming trees sits across the street from their house. We play here a lot. I love running under the trees, feeling the warm breeze brush against my skin, swinging with all my might as high as I can. I have so much fun, and I'm no longer worried about being hungry or scared… or killed.

One day Libby takes us to the community pool. I am so happy we get to go swimming that as soon as we get to the pool, I jump in. What I don't know is that there is a shallow end and a deep end – and of course I pick the wrong end.

If you jump in the deep end, you better know how to swim. I have never learned, so I bob up and down a couple of times until one of the lifeguards comes and rescues me. I swallow a lot of water in the process, and it scares me a bit. After that Libby makes sure I stay in the shallow end.

On another day Libby takes us to the Fernbank Museum. And still another day, we go to the zoo. These are both fascinating places to me. But my favorite trip of all is when she takes us camping on Cumberland Island.

You have to take a ferry to get to the island, and I love the ferry ride. It is slow and peaceful. The wind blows so easily over you, and every so often it brings with it this strange new smell – a salty, swampy smell that most people don't like. But to me it is more interesting than unpleasant, because it suggests we are going to a place unlike any place I've ever been.

Getting off the ferry, we have to walk a little way to our campsite. And on the other side of the campsite is a beach with white sand. The ocean beyond is such a bright blue, covered in glittering sparkles from the sun. And the showers and bathrooms at the campsite are amazing to me as well – yet another piece of this fascinating trip that is full of new and exciting things.

As you might guess, this is the first time I see a beach or the ocean, and the first time I ever go camping. I am so excited that as soon as we get there I run to the beach with my clothes on. I sit down at the edge of the water and take off my pants.

A couple walks by, giving me the funniest look. Then they smile and pull out a camera. I don't know any better… and I certainly don't care. I proceed to shed the rest of my clothes and run naked into the ocean. Libby runs after me, pulls me out of the ocean and puts my clothes back on. She takes me back to the campsite where I discover there is this thing called a swimsuit!

That whole day is awesome. The sparkling ocean, the constant roaring of the waves, the mist spraying you like rain, the wind blowing so hard you can hardly stand up. We walk around the island looking at horses and wild boar and a lot of different kinds of birds unlike any I had ever seen before. The cranes are my favorite, their long graceful necks and wings moving in slow motion as they glide around. And when the sun gets low and red on the horizon, and the sky is a darker, deeper blue-black, we build a campfire.

Afterwards, I am so tired I fall asleep. The next thing I know we are back on the ferry on our way home.

On reflection, what Jerry and Libby did for us is beyond words. Their acts of kindness were an immeasurable sacrifice, a priceless gift. I wish I could tell them how grateful I am to them for sponsoring us, but words aren't enough. All I can do is say, "Thank you, and I love you for what you did for me and my family. You saved our lives." You are both heroes.

After a few months of living with our sponsors, we move into our own house. It is August of 1981.

I don't know where we are exactly, but there are lots of buildings around, so we must be in the city. It is a three-bedroom house with a large front porch and roomy enough for all of us. In fact, Sidan and I even have a room of our own!

A metal gate wraps all the way around our front and back yard. The neighborhood is quiet and peaceful. No one ever bothers us, but despite this, we rarely play outside. We stay in the house most all the time.

With so many of us in the house together, we always have plenty to keep us busy. All my cousins are girls, except for Meanrith; he is Sidan's age. The next three oldest girls – Malis, Moldavy, and Annette – spend most of their time helping Aunt Sim with cooking, cleaning, and everything else that has to be done around the house. I spend most of my time playing with Morokath, who is a year older than me, and Meta, a year younger. My youngest cousin, Alynn, is a toddler, so she stays with Mom most all the time.

My aunt and uncle are now Mom and Dad to me. I know they are my aunt and uncle, of course, but having no living parents, they become my parents. They treat Sidan and me like their own children, and I love them as Mom and Dad.

As a matter of fact, I think they are sometimes even more tolerant and loving toward Sidan and me than they are to their own. Maybe it is because we lost all our family, and they feel sorry for us. Besides, they have six girls and only one boy, and I think they are delighted to *adopt* a couple of boys. At any rate, this is the most normal life has ever been for me.

But "normal" still has its share of adventures… like the day I decide to use a long metal pole to turn off the light switch in our room. Our bedroom light switch does not have a cover on it. So every time I turn it off or on, it bites me. Sometimes it's a little bite, sometimes a bigger bite. One day I decide I've had enough of being bit by the switch, so I find a metal pole about five feet long. This way I figure I can get the job done from a safe distance.

Carefully, I balance my pole well enough to direct it to the light switch. It takes some skill to get it just at the right spot. But just as soon as I push to turn it on, the inevitable happens.

It's as if some force comes out of left field, knocking me backward five feet. The ringing in my ears prevents me from hearing my brother yelling at me. Not only do I take a hit, but the whole area around the switch is now black. It goes without saying that I learn a valuable lesson in electricity that day!

We live in that house for about a year, and then we move to Decatur, a smaller town near Atlanta. This house is on Adair Street. I start first grade at Westchester Elementary School on Scott Boulevard, and we get to ride the bus to school. There is also a park close by that we go to all the time. I love playing in the park because there are other kids there to play with.

I also love climbing all the many crabapple trees that are in the park. My friends love to eat the crabapples, which are too sour for my liking. But I like climbing, so I climb the tree and pick the apples for them.

Another Cambodian couple lives close by. My aunt and uncle spend a lot of time at their house, and they come over to our house a lot, too. Before long, we kids began spending the night at their house. I like that, because they have a TV and we don't.

The most wonderful thing about this year for me is the friends I make in my neighborhood. One of my best friends is Asian. Another is an American boy with curly, blonde hair. His parents are very nice. They always ask me to stay for dinner. I especially like it when his mom cooks spaghetti or fixes sandwiches for us.

Another friend lives about ten houses up the street from us. He has a *Big Wheel* that he rides all the time. I love riding that Big Wheel! His parents must take note of this fact because one day, they surprise me with one. *My very own Big Wheel!*

We live there for about a year or so, and then we move again in the summer when school is out. I hate moving. I especially hate leaving my friends. (I find out later that the reason we keep moving is because the rent goes up every year and my aunt and uncle can't afford the new rate.)

So I start second grade at a new school. And for the first time I run into something I don't understand. Kids at this new school are more standoff-ish. And some of them pick on us. When you walk near them, they shove you, or push you with their elbow, or get in front of you in line.

It is actually a blessing that we barely know any English at this point. This means most of what they say – or the names they call us – don't mean anything to us. We don't understand what is happening, so we decide it must just be something people in America do. And once we're home, we either just stay in our house or play in our yard. We don't go anywhere or try to make new friends.

Besides, considering everything else my aunt and uncle are going through, they don't need us to get into trouble. I pick up on the fact that my best bet is to keep calm, not fight back, and stay focused on school. So that's what I do.

17

Opposite Sides of the World

This is a good time to revisit the fact that as far as my family is concerned, there are yet again two stories running concurrently. Sovannary is still in Camp Seven in Cambodia.

Little do we in America know that she is on the cusp of another tragic experience. This one will catch her utterly by surprise.

Because these events are best suited to a timeline, I'm going to share them with you in this fashion. The words are Sovannary's own:

Camp Seven, April 1981

Now that I know my two brothers are safe with my aunt and uncle and on their way to America, I can focus on what I need to do next.

I have an uncle on my father's side who lives in Canada. His name is Tehm Ung. Uncle Tehm is a well-established dentist in the Canadian province of Quebec. He has been living and working in Canada since before Pol Pot came to power.

Believing this is the best chance my young family has to leave, I write him to see if he will sponsor us. I explain to him that all but three of my family are dead as a result of Cambodia's civil war, including my mother and father.

All I can do now is just wait and hope the letter finds him.

Camp Seven, July 1981

By now my aunt and uncle, cousins, and brothers have arrived in America. Instead of going with them, I made the decision to stay here with my husband, hoping we can leave together as a family when the time comes. After all, Ny Keo is a high-ranking officer in the military organization that runs the camp, so I believe we are relatively safe here.

And then one day, out of the blue, my husband says he must leave.

"WHAT? *Why?*" I asked.

"They want me dead."

We both just stand there.

"*They?* Who are *'they'*?"

The organization Ny Keo belongs to is somewhat like the Mafia in the sense that a few powerful people run things and do whatever they want. Someone with some clout decided they want Ny Keo killed. I don't know why or what the situation is. They just want him killed.

Not only that, Ny Keo's trusted friend is assigned... *commanded*, to do the job!

So under what I can only imagine is unbearable inner conflict, he comes to Ny Keo and, at great risk to himself, tells him: "Brother, you need to go to Thailand. You have to leave tonight because at 10:00 o'clock tomorrow morning I have to come here and kill you."

I don't understand. It's like we are still in a workcamp under the thumb of the Khmer Rouge. I remember telling Sidan this place is a little like the *wild west*, but I thought at least we would be safe because of my husband's position.

"Don't worry," Ny Keo tells me. "I'll figure something out."

"*Like what?*"

"I don't know yet. But for now, I have to go," he said. "I have to leave."

I can't believe what I am hearing.

"I love you," he kisses me. And he's gone.

Camp Seven, August 1981

A few days ago, our baby boy, Tota Ung, was born... in a refugee camp, no less. I am deeply saddened by the fact that his father is not with us for the birth of our first child. But Tota is here now. He is healthy, and I'm recovering well. For these two things I am thankful.

I am completely surprised when, just a few days later, my husband returns. But what does this mean? *Has the threat on his life gone away?*

"I couldn't stay away," he tells me. "It isn't right. Besides, I would rather have only one more day with you and our son than to run away."

He had barely finished this sentence when a portion of his head explodes. He has been shot by someone from somewhere just outside our hut.

And there, right in front of me, my young husband is dead. Ny Keo has just returned to the camp. He barely had a chance to see and hold his newborn son. And now he is dead.

He couldn't stand the thought of having left me, of not being here to protect me, and not being here when our son was born. And now he is gone for good. Once again, somehow, the pages of my life have gotten darker.

It is just so hard to picture this. Sovannary is my older sister, but she is still just a girl living in that same war-torn country. Only now, none of her immediate family is with her. Even her husband can't be with her because, due to an order coming down from higher up that he be murdered, he has had to flee for his life. Consequently, she had to give birth to their first child alone.

Then, because he cannot stand to feel he is neglecting to protect his wife, my brother-in-law returns and is *that very same day* shot in the head and killed. And to multiply the horror, this occurs right in front of Sovannary. It's enough compounded trial and sorrow to shatter your heart.

Sovannary continues with her story:
<u>Khao-I-Dang, February 1982</u>
After Ny Keo was murdered, Tota and I had to stay another five or six months in that awful hell hole before being accepted in Khao-I-Dang. I can't describe what it was like living in the tent where I saw my husband shot and killed. The day we move to Khao-I-Dang is a day of relief!

It's just the two of us now. I must admit I'm lonely and tired, but life is gradually getting better. At least I can see a bit of hope for our future – if only a little – though I have no idea where we will end up.

My cousin, Malis, and I have always been close, so we keep in touch by writing each other. She tells me what life is like in America. She says there are many good things and some not so good. It's wintertime, and she complains about the cold.

The food is quite different, too. Americans eat hamburgers and hot dogs, chips, and soda – *fast food* – they call it. It tastes good, she says, but it's very different. And it doesn't really satisfy.

Their sponsors bring groceries over weekly or bi-weekly. No one in the family knows how to drive, or where to go to buy food, although sometimes they do ride with the sponsor to the grocery store. Malis says the grocery stores are fun to visit, and I agree it seems like they would be. It sounds like freedom!

It seems Malis is having quite a challenge getting adjusted, so I do what I can to encourage her. I know she can learn to adjust. At least no one is dying or starving. *Look at it as the beginning of a whole new life*, I tell her.

The best days are when I get her letters. Sometimes I laugh and sometimes I cry… but I always try to imagine what life is like for all of them. I always end the letter with, "Please take care of my brothers, especially the *swollen* one [Sideth]."

In her return letter she tells me, "Sideth is not swollen anymore. He looks very healthy now, but everybody still calls him *Haem,* out of love, of course."

Even now, no one can believe Sideth survived. Everybody thought for sure he would die along the way, but somehow he made it, and he's doing well. He's growing, and he's in school. Sidan is also in school, and he's working. This is such great news to me. I miss them all so much.

She tells me to let her know when something changes for us. "Don't worry," Malis tells me, "when you get out, we will meet again."

Malis and I write each other for almost two years… from the spring of 1981 to the end of 1982. Her letters keep me going, keep me hopeful during these lonely days and nights.

Tota and I are in Khao-I-Dang for about fourteen months altogether before being accepted to Chon Buri. We are now on the same path my aunt and uncle, cousins and brothers have travelled.

As soon as he got my letter, my uncle Tehm Ung contacted the Canadian government. And after almost two years of waiting, they finally accept his request to sponsor us to Canada.

Tota and I board a plane and go straight to Canada, the province of Quebec. There I meet Uncle Tehm and catch him up on everything that has happened, especially as to how we lost most all our family. He is brokenhearted by the story.

I look outside; there is no ground visible anywhere. Only snow. I have never seen snow before, so you can imagine how strange this all seems.

Then I look around… and I whisper to myself how good it feels to be back with family.

As of January 1983, we are finally free at last!

Even though she is not in Georgia with the rest of us, I am ecstatic that Sovannary and my little nephew are out of Cambodia. *We all are.* Our hearts grieve for her over the loss of Ny Keo. And it saddens us to think that her young son, when he was but days old, lost his father to a murderer's gun.

But they are free now. And even though they are not with us, they are with family. And we take great comfort in that.

It's now 1983, and I'm in second grade at a new school, Hooper Alexander. My fascination with numbers, coupled with the fact that every day while walking to school I pass this mailbox with the numbers "1983" on it, makes this particular year stand out in my mind. And every time I see it, my mind adds up the numbers, which total 21… reminding me of one of the card games my cousins play. Funny how your mind works.

We now live on Colombia Drive. There's a QuickMart across the street and just around the corner from us. I get a lot of joy out of going there. For some reason, I find the store intriguing.

Our house is a typical, three-bedroom ranch style, but smaller than the other two we have lived in. So some of us sleep on the floor. My uncle has the sofa. Since we don't have a car, Sidan and I convert the garage into a room for us. But that's more than okay.

Second grade is also significant to me for another reason. This is the first time I write my name… in any language.

You may wonder why no one taught me to do this sooner, especially in America where it's considered important to know how to write your name. But my aunt and uncle were like a lot of other refugee adults at that time – they didn't interact a lot with us kids.

Besides, they have their hands full trying to keep up a household of 11 and make ends meet. Even though in Cambodia my aunt was a nurse and my uncle a doctor, their credentials do not translate to equivalent positions in America. But they cope very well, which helps the rest of us do the same.

Obviously, we are all thankful to just be alive and that we don't have to run for our life anymore. But now I understand that a big part of their struggle was the anger and frustration over losing everything and having to live in a foreign country without any status or money. Everything they worked so hard for, for so long, disappeared in the blink of an eye. Now they live as refugees, barely scraping by.

And knowing very little English, the only jobs they can find nearby are manufacturing jobs that are unchallenging, given their intellects... jobs they perform almost robotically. They work at a factory that makes belts and suspenders and the like. Nonetheless, they are grateful to have jobs.

As time goes on, they meet other Cambodian refugee families. They get together and tell stories. They laugh and cry and sometimes there's an obviously bitter side to their conversations.

And why not? Though they are careful to keep everything in perspective, you can hear in their voices and their descriptions of what happened in Cambodia just how they suffered, and how much they lost.

However, for having to start over completely from scratch, our family manages to do well with what we have. Everybody who can work does – and pitches in on expenses.

I even do some work for our next-door neighbor, an old man who lives alone. One day I see him chopping wood, and I go over and help him move the log he had just cut. I'm not sure if he asks me to help, or if I ask him if I could help, but when we are done, he gives me a quarter.

And after saving up a few quarters of earnings, I go shopping at the QuickMart. Rationalizing that my quarters can't help that much anyway, I buy me some bubblegum!

Later that year my oldest cousin, Malis, marries a Cambodian guy. We roast a pig in the backyard to celebrate, which is pretty cool! Naturally she moves out of the house, and after that we don't see her as much. Malis has been such a big part of our story to date and though happy for her, we all miss her.

The best thing about 1983 and second grade has not yet happened though. But it's just around the corner....

18

A Teacher with a Mother's Heart

By now you no doubt agree with me that Providence always shows up in my life when I need it most. I am about to share another of those situations with you, this time in the form of a woman who completely changes my life. She is easily one of the kindest, most loving, most amazing people I have ever met.

This lady is a teacher – my second-grade teacher, in fact. She shows just the kind of impact a teacher can have on a life. Her name is Regina Hughes and, as you may have guessed, she is *certainly* a hero of mine!

I want you to hear from Mrs. Hughes in her own words:

> At the end of the Vietnam War, Georgia State University contacted me and three other elementary teachers to enlist our help with the many Vietnamese refugees coming into the Atlanta area.
>
> I couldn't bear the thought of any one of them not being welcomed, so I was thrilled to be a part of this effort and I accepted every child they sent me. I also attended Georgia State that summer and the next year until I completed an English to Speakers of Other Languages (ESOL) certification.
>
> These students were bussed to Garden Hills Elementary School in Buckhead. In addition to some basic lessons in culture and linguistics, one of our initial responsibilities in this 20-hour pre-classroom orientation program was to teach them how to

wear shoes. You see, every one of them – whether from Vietnam, Cambodia, or Laos – had gone barefoot all their life.

But introducing them to the concept of wearing shoes was not our greatest challenge. We also had to get them accustomed to the idea of wearing underwear. For a while, every time we tried, they would throw those garments back at us over the bathroom stalls!

One day while teaching at Hooper Alexander School in Dekalb County, two new students were brought to my class. The girl was Morokath Mam. Morokath's nuclear family was still intact, and she seemed quite well adjusted. The other student was Morokath's cousin, Sideth Ung. Sideth had come from Cambodia with his brother and Morokath's family.

I'll never forget Sideth's very first words to me on that very first day. He looked up at me with such innocent eyes and said, *"No Mama. No Papa."*

That's all it took! I determined at that moment that I would do everything I could to make up for what this little boy had lost.

To begin with, he had an older pair of adult tennis shoes sort of 'tied' around his feet. And his pants and shirt were both ragged... and way too small. His pant legs ended about midway up his shins and had big holes in them. So I knew right away where we needed to start.

Mrs. Hughes, my new second-grade teacher at this new school, is a very nice lady. And what I am about to find out is that she is yet another one of those many angels God brings into my life now and again to get me through another hard stretch.

Every day in class she teaches me a new word that she calls our "word of the day." She tells me the word, and when I ask what it means she always says, "Look it up." It is like a game, and of course it helps me learn.

Then one day she picks a word that I thought was kind of strange. The word was: *shopping.*

"What does it mean?" I ask.

This time instead of telling me to look it up, she says "I will tell you later." So, I go back to my schoolwork. A few days later she picks me up from our house and takes me to a store and buys me a new pair of green Nike tennis shoes – the kind with the checkmark on the side. I feel like a million bucks in my new shoes! Walking out of the store, Mrs. Hughes looks at me and smiles and says, *"that's shopping!"*

She continues:

> Because of my certification, I get permission to visit Sideth's home. When I see where he is living and how things are there, I have a much better picture of how our family can help him. I had taught three refugees before, Asian refugees that were all from the same family. But their family unit was intact. And when the family is intact, you see a totally different situation. They are very, very thankful to be in America and very excited about everything.
>
> But Sideth has almost nothing. Sidan, his only other sibling here, is a full eight years older. And although their aunt and uncle are to be commended for incorporating their two nephews into their family, they have seven children of their own. So 11 people are living here under this one roof.
>
> Even with the financial support they receive from the Catholic Relief Services Organization and what meager monies they make working factory jobs, it is all they can do to keep food on the table. Affording clothing for them all is another matter altogether. Not only that, both Sidan and Sideth are sleeping on a mattress on the floor in the garage because again, space and resources are so limited.
>
> So the evening after our shopping trip I go home and tell my son, Peter, about Sideth. "There's a very nice young fella who's new to my classroom, but he desperately needs clothes. He's about your size," (Sideth was born in 1972 and Peter in 1971). "So why don't we sit down together and see what you might like to share with him…" and then I open the drawers of his dresser.
>
> Peter is so generous. "I like these pants, but he can have these. I'd like to keep this shirt…" We go through Peter's entire dresser and when we are done, we have gathered a large bag full of clothes to give Sideth.

Somewhere around the middle of my second-grade year my stomach starts bothering me regularly. It feels a little like I'm hungry, but I'm not. I feel this sharp pain that really hurts and then a few minutes later it's gone. It hurts worse at night, so I start sleeping with a pillow pressed up against my stomach trying to ease the pain.

Sometimes I go for a couple months at a time without it hurting, but then it comes back and lasts for a week or more.

I figure that I have some kind of disease, but I don't tell anybody. My aunt and uncle have enough troubles without having to worry about me. I think my brother knows though, because it turns out that he has the same problem.

One thing I know for sure is that I do not want to go to the hospital. My real mom died in a hospital.

This goes on until I get so worried that I finally tell my aunt about it. She was, after all, a nurse. She says it is an ulcer and that it will probably cause me problems for years to come.

But besides the ulcer, and the occasional bullying at school, my life now is pretty much the same as anyone else's. We go to school, the adults go to work, and in the evenings we either play or watch TV.

We now have a black-and-white TV that requires a pair of pliers to change the channel because the selector is broken. The only problem is there are 11 of us – young kids and older kids and adults. Naturally we fight over what shows we watch. The younger kids want to watch cartoons. The older kids and adults want soap operas.

So whenever we don't get to watch what I want to watch, I go outside in the backyard and play in the creek until dinnertime. And that suits me just fine.

19

Making Up for Lost Time

Not long after my teacher, Mrs. Hughes, took me shopping, I find out that I'm in for another treat. One day Mrs. Hughes asked my aunt and uncle for permission to take me home with her on Friday for the weekend so her son, Peter, and I can play together. *I have no idea at the time, but from this day on, my life will forever change.* What a gift lay in store for me!

Here is how Mrs. Hughes tells it:

> Because we all like being together so much, Sideth starts staying with us over the summers and for Christmas and spring and fall breaks. We are careful to make sure he is still very much a part of his aunt and uncle's family, of course. That way they continue to qualify for the $350 every month from Catholic Charities USA, money which they so desperately need.

The first day I meet Peter, he is sitting on the floor in their living room watching TV. Whatever he is watching is so funny that he laughs so hard he throws up what he's been eating and drinking all over the floor! Talk about an introduction!

Right out of the gate, Peter and I are the best of friends. He sees me as just another kid from the neighborhood. He has no idea I am a Cambodian refugee from a ghetto neighborhood that his mom picks up from this ghetto school.

I still don't speak that much English, so we don't talk at lot at first. But he is patient with me and shows me how to play with whatever toys or games he chooses. Sometimes we play cowboys and Indians, and other times we build things with PlayDoh and Tinker Toys and blocks that hook together.

He also has this machine that looks like a TV that you can play games on called a Commodore 64 computer. All he has to do is put this flat square disk into a slot on the computer, type a few letters on the keyboard, and we can play. We play all kinds of games… but my favorites are Pong and Breakout.

Then Peter gets this other machine called Atari. It looks different from the computer but works basically the same. We play games on that thing all day long – Asteroids, Centipedes, Dig Dug, Galaxian, Hang Man, Joust, Pac-Man (my favorite), Frogger, and Mario Brothers.

Peter has a lot of very cool toys that he shares with me. Sometimes he even gives me toys to take home – like a bow and arrow set (with stoppers instead of arrowheads), a skateboard, Matchbox cars, and more. I never had toys of my own before so you can imagine how special this makes me feel!

I also get Peter's clothes when he outgrows them. I can't tell you how this simple act of goodness impacts my life. For the first time since coming to America I can actually dress cool, look good, and fit in.

And as a direct result of all this, sometime deep into the second grade, *a new Sideth begins to emerge.* I had no idea what a difference having nice clothes would do to affect the way I feel about myself. I am confident. I feel like one of the kids in the neighborhood… *his* neighborhood, not mine.

Then one day Peter asks me what I want for Christmas.

"Christmas?" I have no idea what that is. *"What do you mean what do I want?"*

"You know… what do you want for Christmas?" he repeated.

"I don't know. Besides, what's Christmas?"

Peter proceeds to tell me all about Christmas. He tells me about Santa and the fact that on the night before Christmas he brings presents to your house and eats the cookies you leave for him on the table.

I think he's crazy. And I still don't know what to ask for. But he keeps on asking me. I finally remember a commercial about a remote-control tank. Yeah… that's what I want.

And that's what I get that Christmas!

I'm like, "What's going on? And who is this Santa guy again?"

And then the next thing I know, Peter says, "Hey Sed, what do you want for your birthday?" It's too much... but I sure like it!

But then I remember this miniature racetrack I saw on TV that glows in the dark. You put this track together... you can even put it up on the wall... and lo and behold, the car will drive up the wall! It has some kind of magnet that keeps the car on the track.

Wouldn't you know it, a couple of days later – on February 2, 1984 – I am the proud new owner of that indoor racetrack!

You might be wondering what my aunt and uncle, brother and cousins all think about how much time I spend with the Hughes' family.

I wondered that too, so when I go home one afternoon after being at Peter's house, I talk to Aunt Sim about it. The conversation starts when I tell her about some new toy they get me.

Aunt Sim is so understanding. She makes sure I know she doesn't mind me going to their house and getting things; she doesn't mind at all. As long as I am happy, my aunt and uncle and everyone else are all happy for me. I have always thought that this shows the kind of people my aunt, uncle, and cousins are. It would be so easy, especially for my cousins, to be bitter or jealous over my good fortune.

I am having a blast now in America. As you can imagine, all the exciting distractions make it possible for me to not think much about what happened to me and my family in Cambodia and everything I have lost. Sure, I still think about all that from time to time. And when I do, I get angry and sad. I feel lost and alone.

But thankfully that doesn't happen often. I am so busy now with school and with Peter and his family that my mind just slowly moves away from all that to the present and whatever is coming next... which includes summertime.

Now that school is out, I get to spend I lot more time with Peter and his family – a lot more than we did during the school year even.

The caveat is that we have to read. Everywhere we go that summer, and no matter what else we are doing, Mrs. Hughes puts a book in my hand and expects me to read it. Sometimes she has me read to her, and sometimes I read to myself. And every time I finish one book, she has another one ready. I catch on to what she is doing by about the third book.

More importantly though, and quite to my advantage, whenever I finish a book, she gives me a dollar. *You mean I get paid for reading?* So I read and I read, every chance I get. I jump headfirst into Mrs. Hughes' never-ending library of books. She takes Peter and me to the library and we sit there for hours and just read. Sometimes I read in the car, and other times we have "quiet time" at their house and do nothing but read.

Most of the books I read are children's books with big letters, and books with lots of pictures and just a few words. One of my favorites is a book about all kinds of different animals and their occupations, by an author named Richard Scarry. Every animal has their special place and their tasks to perform. This bustling city of animals looks like such fun!

My favorite book of all time though, is about a boy who lives out in the country with his mom. He is about 11 years old, but he has no friends. Every time he gets in trouble, he goes into the woods where there is a pool of water – a pond or a lake or something. He jumps in and swims under the water and comes out on the other side of the world. And in this new world, he has special powers. He can jump high and run fast and do anything he wants to do. Everyone in the new world likes him because he is their superhero, helping other people with his special powers.

Sometimes Peter rides his bike to my house and brings his skateboard. We play for a while, and then I ride his bike back to his house, pulling him on his skateboard behind me.

We also spend a lot of time at a community pool during the summer. I love the water, but I still don't know how to swim so I stay at the shallow end most of the time (as you remember, I nearly drowned *twice* before).

Peter swims like a fish. One day he had had enough of me not knowing how to swim, so he tries teaching me. I am scared, but he is persistent. He shows me how to swing my arms back and forth. After a few strokes I start sinking, and he pulls me back up and we try again, only for the same thing to happen again. Then after a few frustrating tries, he pushes me into the pool and says, *"Stroke... stroke... stroke!"* In just a few minutes I am floating and swimming, or sort of, in the shallow end of the pool.

I get more and more confident as I keep swinging my arms back and forth and kicking my feet. Peter is right there, helping me stay afloat. And before I know it, I am swimming! After a couple of weeks, I feel like an Olympian!

During that first summer, Mrs. Hughes takes Peter and me to her sister's house. Her sister, Athelia, has two kids – Jonathan Jordan and Don Jordan, a.k.a. JJ and DJ.

Before long, Peter and I start spending weekends with them. Then pretty soon, I go alone and stay with them. After that, you can bet that if I'm not with Peter, I'm with JJ.

Being with Peter is a lot different than being with JJ. Peter is rowdy, kind of crazy, and rough… whereas JJ is quieter and a lot more orderly.

As an example, one day Peter gets this new beanbag chair. He has this brilliant idea of setting the beanbag against the wall and having me run toward it. Peter stations himself at the midway point, more or less, and when I reach him, he picks me up and throws me onto the beanbag. Great idea, right?

Well, we fail to adjust for velocity and distance and so on, so I either land on the floor or flat against the wall. After a number of tries, a few bruises, and a decidedly dizzy feeling, I say, "I give up. It's your turn!"

At JJ's though, activities are more sedate, and even run on a schedule. We wake up at a certain time and his mom makes us breakfast, and then we watch some TV, mostly cartoons. Then we go outside and play, come back, have lunch, and play outside again.

In the evening, after dinner we go downstairs with his boombox and his cassettes. One of our favorites is a hip-hop group called Run DMC. He cranks the music up and starts to dance. He tells me it's called *break-dancing*. I give it a try, but at that very moment I discover that I don't have a dancing bone in my body.

JJ, by contrast, has this move called *the windmill*. He spins on his back and then stops with one foot crossed over the other. He is amazing.

Right before bedtime, we have some down time, which JJ uses for drawing. Boy is he talented! He does what he calls *grafitti drawing* where he makes words jump out at you. I can sit for hours watching him draw, night after night. I am even more amazed at his drawing than his dancing.

Later that summer Mrs. Hughes takes Peter and me for a long road trip to see our *Nanny and Papa* for summer vacation. I have no idea who our Nanny and Papa are, but I am glad to be going just the same.

Nanny and Papa live in Florida, in a small town by the St. John's River. Their home is this neat little wooden house situated right on the river and is equipped with a dock and a boat. Across the road from their house is this huge orange orchard.

Peter got to bring his Atari with him, so some of the time we play Atari. But most of the time we spend outside, just being kids.

Papa is a very prompt, early-bird sort of person, and a stickler at that. He gets up very early in the morning and cooks a big, hearty breakfast – but you have to be there for it or you miss out. When I say big, I mean bacon, eggs, grits, pancakes, fruit, and everything in between.

Of course, Peter and I oversleep most of the time and miss it. But at other times Papa is kind enough to come in and splash cold water on our faces to get us out of bed. (Trust me, it works!)

Papa walks around with a cane, and if you misbehave, he won't hesitate to use it. We never got any licks from it, however, so apparently just the thought of it is strong enough to keep us on the straight and narrow.

Some mornings, if we get up early enough, we can have breakfast and go fishing. Papa cooks a mean fish fry, I'll tell ya! (I still have not had a fish fry better than his!)

On other days we play around the house until the sun is high, and then we go swimming. And occasionally we go water skiing.

One day Papa announces that we are headed for a different adventure when it gets dark enough. We are going to catch alligators! At first, I don't believe him. I am fascinated, but I have no idea why we want to hunt alligators at night, especially when alligators have big mouths and sharp teeth that they can eat you with!

But lo and behold, night falls, and here we go. The three of us out in a boat – a funny little boat, the kind somebody has to pedal. We have nothing more than a flashlight and a wooden pole with a loop of metal wire attached to the front of it.

Peter gets in the back so he can pedal. I get in the middle, and Papa is in the front with the pole. Then Papa says to me: "You see, son… see those two glow-spots over yonder?" Of course, I have no idea what *yonder* means, but I've learned that you can sometimes figure out what a word means by how it's used. So I assume "yonder" meant something like "there."

"Yes," I answer.

"That's an alligator."

So those glow-spots are the eyes of an alligator!

Slowly, Peter pedals our boat toward these two glow-spots. We get closer, and Papa says to Peter: "You have to go slower, son; you'll scare it away." (All the while I'm thinking to myself, "Then let's go faster!")

We try on several occasions to approach an alligator in the proper way, but we never manage. And I must admit, I thank God we never do. I'm not a real fan of the notion of catching alligators!

We discover at some point that Nanny has a shotgun – a 12-gauge with a lot of "kick" when you shoot it. And now we have another activity to engage in at Nanny and Papa's. Of course, either Nanny or Papa always supervises us!

Sometimes we shoot skeet – discs made of clay that you throw into the air – and sometimes we just shoot into the river. Peter takes aim, and then says, "Look… fish…!" *BOOM!*

Never a dull moment with Peter. But he is FUN – a lot of fun.

And yet, despite all the fun we are having and all there is to occupy us, we decide one day that we are bored – within earshot of Papa. That isn't an issue for long however, because Papa has the perfect solution to this kind of problem. He has us dig a hole, and when we are done, he tells us to fill it back up.

I think we dug a couple more before figuring out Papa's underlying principle. We resolve to never again say that we are bored, or act like we are bored, around Papa… ever, ever, again!

We end the vacation with Nanny and Papa on a high note when the last night, rather late, Peter and I sneak out into the orange orchard across the road. Our brilliant idea is to have an orange fight with some big, juicy, perfectly good oranges… and somehow, we get away with it.

After being at *Camp Nanny-and-Papa* for two full weeks, Peter has to go home. But then it is JJ's turn – and I get to stay one more whole week with JJ.

It is awesome! These three weeks are simply the best vacation I have ever had! I have such a great experience in fact that, by the time I get back home, I can't even explain it all to my aunt and uncle.

20

The Lost and Found

One day toward the end of summer Peter and I are sitting on the front porch steps talking about what to do next when, out of the blue, he says, "Sed, why don't you call my mom, *Mom?*"

"But, she's not my mom."

"Yeah, but you're like a brother to me," he says. "You're my brother now – *Brother.*"

Then, almost as if it had been planned out beforehand, the phone rings. "You should go answer it," Peter says.

I had never answered a phone before, so naturally I'm a little hesitant. "What do I say?"

"When you pick up, just say, 'Hughes residence.'"

So that's what I do. Someone on the other end asks, "Is your mom home?"

I don't know if I even answer them, but I go back outside and tell Peter.

"She's in her room," Peter says. "Call up to Mom and tell her she's got a phone call."

So I went back inside and yell, "Mom!"

And she replies, "Yes, son!"

"Phone call for you!"

And from that day onward, she is no longer Mrs. Hughes to me; she is Mom. I truly feel like I belong and that I have another new family now.

Peter's dad is Jim Hughes – *Dad* to us both now. Dad never has a lot to say. He works during the day, of course. And in the evening, he reads his newspaper and watches the 6:30 evening news. He does yardwork and sometimes helps Mom get dinner ready. Even when he is around, he never talks much; he is just a very quiet, private man.

When he does speak to Peter and me, it is about making sure we do things properly and in order, like brushing our teeth and picking up after ourselves. He also makes sure we behave well, especially when we are in public. He teaches us good manners and the importance of respecting others.

He also teaches us how to pray and be thankful. He never misses praying before a meal, whether we are in public or in the privacy of our home. If Dad is there, we pause to give thanks before we eat. He also reads the Bible and prays with us before bedtime, like clockwork.

Dad works as a Certified Financial Planner at an insurance and annuity firm associated with the *Presbyterian Church in America*. And when he isn't at work, he loves photographing flowers and birds and butterflies and all sorts of animals. He even made a book containing all his pictures.

Sarah is also a member of the Hughes' family – Peter's older sister. When we were younger, she filled the role of babysitter. She often takes us to see a movie, or shopping, sometimes to the arcade, or just to lunch. One time she and a friend even took Peter and me to Panama City Beach.

Then mysteriously, Sarah is no longer around. One day not long after I realize she's gone, Mom packs Peter and me in a car and we go for a drive to a college campus – Auburn University. As it turns out, this is where Sarah was *hiding*. She is now in college. (Later she will transfer and graduate from Emory University.)

At some point during third grade, Mom and Dad sign Peter and me up for the Boy Scouts of America. The highest rank you can earn in the Boy Scouts is Eagle Scout. One of the ways you earn that rank is by participating in outdoor adventures like backpacking, swimming, camping, hiking, and gliding. I do okay in Boy Scouts, but I never make Eagle Scout.

That isn't DJ's fault, however. DJ does everything he can to help me become an Eagle Scout by getting me to go on hikes with him, in both the country as well as the city. Once he took me to Jacks River, and we hiked to this beautiful waterfall. That trip did earn me a hiking badge, however.

One of my favorite Boy Scout adventures was to Kilpatrick Farm where we learn how to build a fire. We also shoot guns and play capture-the-flag.

In our Boy Scout troop, Peter and I have nicknames: Salt and Pepper – because of our first initials, S and P... and because we are always together.

Mom also enrolls me at the YMCA where I try to play basketball. It doesn't take long, however, to find out that basketball is not my strong suit!

Between 1984 and 1985, we move again to a small duplex apartment in an area called Chamblee. We later rename the place *Chambodia!* Every apartment has the exact same style and layout, reminding us of a refugee camp.

A multitude of ethnicities live here – other Asians, as well as whites, Mexicans, and blacks. This place is pretty rough – rougher than any other place we've lived since coming to America.

A couple months after moving here, someone tries to burn our apartment down. They don't finish the job however, because my aunt and uncle discover what they are doing and chase them away. No matter how rough things get though, we survive. And we can thank Cambodia and the Khmer Rouge for toughening us up. There's not much we find daunting after what we've been through!

Third grade is awesome. I have some great friends and get along with almost everyone. And I do okay academically. I'm naturally good in math and fascinated by history. But English gives me a run for my money. So many rules! Words that are spelled the same can have entirely different meanings. And other words that are spelled differently actually sound the same. I struggle with singular and plural nouns, possessive nouns, and proper nouns. And please don't ask me to conjugate my verbs!

Despite my struggles with English, however, third grade is a good year. It goes so well, in fact, that before I know it, summer is already here again. And this summer brings an adventure of a very different kind.

"We're going to Canada," my aunt announces one day, "to see your sister!"

"*What?*"

I am *dumbfounded* – a lot more than you might think. I know I have a sister, but anything I might remember about her is from so long ago, and a place that is so different – a place no one has even spoken about since we left there.

And I never tried remembering that life, once we got to America. I think instinctively and unconsciously I want to forget that all those events ever happened to me. I just want to keep moving forward.

Apparently, I'm not the only one. We never talk about it at home, so I can only assume everyone else in my family wants to forget those times as well.

"Wait… is that the sister we left in Camp Seven?"

"Yes! That's her!"

Apparently, Aunt Sim and Malis have kept in touch with her all this time. But at this point in my life, I barely relate to the idea of a sister (other than my female cousins) – let alone this place called Canada.

I thought Peter might be able to clue me in on Canada. So one day when we are hanging out, I ask him about it.

"Hey, Peter, where's Canada?"

He doesn't know, and he doesn't know anything about it either. So we get out a map and look it up.

The next thing I know, Aunt Sim, Malis, Moldavy, Sidan, and I are headed for Canada. A friend of the family is kind enough to drive us.

On our way, we stop to buy fried chicken for lunch. But instead of eating at the restaurant, we get it to go, and wait until we get to a rest area where there is a pavilion and benches for eating and relaxing.

There are plenty of empty benches, but for some reason my aunt and cousins don't want to sit there. So we all walk way out to the back of the rest area, find a flat, shady, grassy area, and that's where we have lunch.

About five or ten minutes later, as we are enjoying our lunch, we spot a man walking in our direction. He's white, and as he gets closer, we notice he is wearing hippie-type clothes. He has hair down his neck and a full-grown beard. And he is very skinny.

He comes right up to us and asks if he can join us.

"Of course!"

We are happy to have him sit with us.

We offer him some food, but he says that he brought his own. He smiles a lot… just sits with us and smiles. Nothing much is said because none of the adults speak English very well.

After a little more sitting and staring and smiling, one of us asks if we can take a picture with him, and we do. And the next thing we know, he walks away.

I wonder to myself… does an angel ever make an appearance in the guise of a hippie?

It takes us a little over a day to get to Sovannary's house in Canada. When I am introduced to her, it feels awkward. I feel a little guilty that I don't know her or feel anything special toward her when I see her.

So I just give her a typical "hello," like you do when meeting someone for the first time. Truthfully, I don't remember her at all. So of course, I feel no emotion on seeing her again.

She, on the other hand, is very emotional. She keeps pinching me as if she is trying to make sure I am real. She and my aunt and Malis talk – *a lot*. I guess they have a lot of catching up to do. And in the process, they cry a lot too.

Tota, Sovannary's son who was born in the refugee camp in Cambodia, is now about three years old. So of course, my aunt and cousins are excited to see him too.

One day while we are there, we go shopping at the mall. Sovannary takes me around and introduces me to everyone she knows. We also visit our uncle Tehm Ung's home. He is the uncle who sponsored Sovannary and her son.

That was the first of several visits to Canada. And sometimes she and Tota and Uncle Tehm visit us. I'm thankful that my aunt, and especially Malis, kept in touch with her. Otherwise, I may never have seen my sister again.

In late 1986 we move again to another apartment complex that is inside Highway 285, the perimeter highway that goes around Atlanta. I'm now in fifth grade at Nancy Creek Elementary School.

Remember all those books I had to read during summer vacations with my mom? Well, not only did she pay me for each book I read then, but that exercise is continuing to pay off. My fifth-grade teacher, Mrs. Robinson, says that I read well for a fifth grader. "You're doing so well in fact, that we're going to let you skip a grade."

The next thing I know I'm suddenly in sixth grade. What strikes me most about this move to sixth grade is that I am officially not a little kid anymore. This is middle school!

Not long after that, we move yet again. This time it is somewhere way out in Gwinnett County. We are so far out of the city in fact, that there are no streetlights. I don't like it at all, but at least we aren't all scrunched together in a tiny apartment. This time we move into a house.

Something else helps too. Between the last move and this one Sidan gets married and is now living with his wife and her mother. Gradually, as a result of marriages, our *in-house* family is getting smaller and smaller.

But what I hate most about this last move is the fact that I lose contact with Mom, Dad, and Peter. I'm certain now that she has no idea where I am. We have no internet and no cell phones, so I have no way to get in touch with her. And even if I did, we live so far apart now that picking me up is no longer convenient.

Not only do I feel like this last move took us completely off the grid, it also hit me one day how much life has changed from those days with my Hughes' family, Nanny and Papa, summer vacations, Christmas toys, and whole days spent doing nothing but playing games. All those memories now seem odd and out of place – almost like they were from another lifetime. This feels like yet another loss.

But as you know, my life has been defined around losing people I love. So I try to keep looking forward. That's the only way I know to do life.

Sixth grade turns into seventh. And my cousin Alynn, the baby of the family, graduates to the second grade.

One day Alynn comes home with a little sticky note. It reads something like this:

> *Sideth,*
> *This is Mom. Is Alynn Mam your cousin? If so, I'd like to know*
> *where you are living?*
> *Please write down your address and give it to Alynn.*

Well… what do you know? Good ol' Mom! What a *fantastic* surprise!

I write down our address and send it to her by way of Alynn, just as requested.

It's not long until I see Mom again and when I do, she tells the story of events as experienced from her end:

> One day the principal brought me another new student. When she wrote her name on a piece of paper for me and I saw the surname *Mam*, I immediately asked her if she is related to Morokath and Meta (cousins of Sideth whom I also taught), and Sideth Ung. She smiled shyly at me and said, "Yes, and you are Mrs. Hughes."

I am so thrilled… and thankful that once again Providence has come to my aid. Somehow – for whatever reason and by whatever means, out of so many possibilities and so many places we could have moved to, so many schools my cousin could have gone to, and so many teachers she could have had – Alynn *happened* to walk into Mom's class.

And the next thing I know, Mom shows up at our house… and just like that we are back in each other's lives again.

After being apart for a year, Peter starts picking me up for holidays, mostly Thanksgiving and Christmas. He is driving now, which facilitates our getting to be together. (Our family still doesn't have a car.)

Being with Peter again is awesome. It is as wonderful as always… like we had never said goodbye. And come to think of it, we never did!

The next couple of years are normal enough. I meet a new friend who lives a few houses up in the same neighborhood as my family. He moved to America with his family from Odessa, Ukraine, when he was only four. We become great friends, especially after I help him back down some bullies (something I had gotten pretty good at doing).

In 1988, Sidan buys a three-bedroom house on our street, between our house and where my friend lives. It is just Sidan, his wife, and his mother-in-law. To ease money and space pressures on our family, I move in with them and have a room all to myself. This is the first time I've ever had my own room, so this is awesome!

My friend and I sometimes play pool at the local pool hall. We also play cards. One day we are so bored that we decide to play cards with a twist… the loser has to take a shot of vodka.

Now, I am not your best card player. So before we are all done, I get quite dizzy. It takes me over an hour to walk home... which is a good thing, because by the time I get home most of the symptoms from being drunk have worn off and so my family never find out.

Another day when we are at his house, he shows me his dad's magnum handgun. I take it, look it over, and like a real gunslinger, point it at his parents' bed with the end of the barrel right up against the bed. Foolishly, I pull the trigger.

Yep, it was loaded!

We look at each other quite wide-eyed... and then do what we can to hide the bullet hole. I don't know if his parents found out, but we never heard anything about it.

But our wildest escapade is when he shows up at my house in his mom's car. (Both of us had just gotten our driver's permits.)

My friend says, "Let's go for a driving test." He leaves her car running in the driveway, so I figure he means business. "C'mon, I'll let you drive," he says.

I foolishly agree and get behind the wheel. I drive around the neighborhood for a little while, and then go onto the main road, turn into a different neighborhood, and circle back around. When I turn left out of that neighborhood back onto the main road, I nearly hit a van head on!

In all these situations I know God is watching out for me. So much could have gone so wrong so fast. But it didn't. And for that, I am so very grateful.

Because my aunt and uncle's grocery money has to stretch well beyond normal to feed them and all us kids, we never ate much meat while I lived with them. But early one spring weekend, Sidan, my friend, and I take a drive up to some farm in the country. The farmer is out in the field working, so we get out and, with Sidan leading the way, walk up to him and exchange hellos. Sidan takes over and does all the talking from there.

Before long, the farmer calls over some guy to drive a pickup truck out to the pasture of cows, hauling the four of us in the back. Once we get there, Sidan points out the cow he wants (how he could tell one from another was a mystery to me). The farmer tells the driver to stop.

And right then and there that very morning we butcher that cow.

Sidan did most of the work, of course, drawing from his experience back in Cambodia. We then wrap and pack the meat and put it in ice-filled coolers. When we get back home, we put the meat in the freezer. That beef lasts us for a good half year!

My friend and I become as close as family. I think the fact that we are both immigrants really drew us together. The summer before high school, in fact, he got to go to Canada with us to visit my sister. (And wouldn't you know, we are still friends to this day.)

The only real downside in my life between elementary and high school is the fact that my ulcer continues to flare up from time to time. So in my teen years, I am in and out of the emergency room periodically on those occasions when it gets inflamed. Every time I go in, they always tell me the same thing. Then they give me a prescription and send me on my way.

I find out some while later that both Sidan and Sovannary have the same problem. It's no wonder.

But life goes on. Summer is now over, and high school is about to begin. And that is a whole other ball of wax.

21

Ebbs and Flows of Life

It's late summer of 1989, and I'm smack in the middle of all the other *green* freshmen at Meadowcreek High School, the new high school in my neighborhood. Meadowcreek first opened in 1986 to relieve the overcrowding of neighboring schools, so it still has that *new school* feel to it.

Almost everyone I went to middle school with ended up at one of the other high schools, but that doesn't bother me. In fact, I fit right into the diverse student population at Meadowcreek. It is mainly Caucasian, but there are a lot of nationalities represented in the student body.

The latter factor usually leads to subgroups and social cliques. But I don't pay attention to that kind of thing. I prefer to hang out with pretty much everyone.

The way I see it, most of those differences disappear once you really get to know somebody anyway. And if you give a person a chance, you will find something you like about them that you can begin to build a friendship on.

Since we live in the same neighborhood, my Ukrainian buddy is also at Meadowcreek. I am thrilled by that fact. We make friends with a guy from Vietnam who came to America about the same time as I did. I also make other friends – mainly from Eastern European countries such as Romania, Russia, Poland, Bosnia, and Serbia.

We all relate to each other because we are all either immigrants or refugees. And we all have a common bond it turns out. *War stories.* For this reason, some of these same guys become friends for life. Such a shared history makes for a *powerful* attachment!

Since I love sports and competing so much, one of the first things I want to do in high school is to try out for a team. I am no good at basketball, so the obvious choices are wrestling and football – even though I only weigh about a hundred pounds soaking wet. As it turns out, I qualify for both options, so I get to pick my poison. The football gear is free, and the wrestling uniform is not. So football it is!

Truth be told, the sport I really want to play is soccer, but Meadowcreek doesn't have a freshman soccer team. We play a little soccer in PE, though. And when my PE teacher sees what I can do on the soccer field, he lets me try out for the varsity team. And I make it!

But I only get to play a few games before my high school soccer career comes to an abrupt end – due to a broken ankle. My teammates tag me with the nickname "Peg Leg," because I'm in a cast for the rest of the season.

As to academia, I like learning in general. I just never could understand how some kids can sleep through class and still get all A's, while I have to study like a madman for B's and C's. That makes me a bit jealous, to be honest.

Peter is a couple years ahead of me in school, and he is now in college at Georgia Tech. He moved out of Mom and Dad's to live with JJ in the Little Five Points area. Little Five Points is a very artsy, bohemian kind of neighborhood not far from downtown Atlanta. I visit them on occasion, when I have some extra time.

And Peter isn't the only one in the family to move that year. Nanny and Papa sell their home on the St. Johns River in Florida and buy a home in Arlington, Georgia.

The summer before my sophomore year Peter and I take a trip to Arlington to visit them. They have a pecan farm, a pool, and plenty of open yard to ride Peter's dirt bike around in, which we take full advantage of.

One day Peter hops in Papa's old Mazda pickup truck that is parked in the driveway and says, "Let's go, Sed. I'm going to teach you how to drive Papa's truck."

"*What?!?* It's a stick shift – I can't drive that thing!"

"It's no different than the dirt bike," he said: "You have the clutch, the brake, and the gas."

Fortunately, Arlington only has one stop light. And there are more trees than cars – although avoiding trees is a good idea, too.

"Okay, but you know Papa will beat us with his cane if we break it," I say, half joking.

Peter drove first, all the while giving me directions. "Left foot on the clutch, right foot on either the brake or the gas. If your right foot is on the brake, your left foot should be holding the clutch down. And when you let go of the clutch, just give it some gas. Listen to the engine; it should be humming steadily. If it makes a shrieking sound…"

By this point I am so lost. You know how sometimes people rattle on and on and expect you to absorb everything they're saying? That's where I am.

So now it's my turn.

Clonk…clonk…

"Give it some gas," Peter says. "Don't be afraid to give it some gas."

I give it some gas alright, and it leaps and takes off like a shot. So I put on the brake – without remembering to also put the other foot on the clutch at the same time – and it *clonks* again.

Unfortunately, Peter is both patient… and persistent. After all, this is his idea and he's not going to give it up so easily. "Slowly…" he says. "Feel the movement of the truck… and when it's moving at the right speed, and it sounds right… slowly let off the clutch and give it more gas."

I try several more times, but a straight shift just isn't my forte. At my insistence, Peter agrees to let us leave it at that.

By the next summer Nanny and Papa move again. This time they move into a neat little home in the middle of Atlanta, in the Peachtree Corners area. It reminds me of a cabin, surrounded by trees. Now I don't have to travel so far to visit them, which is awesome!

My junior year I decide to move sports off the table, as work and school are my focus now. I am busy preparing myself for the *real world*, so to speak.

My only other consideration is girls. Not that I date; I don't even go to the junior prom!

I adore girls though, and so I hang out with them… *a lot.* I just don't have the guts to ask one out. If ever I muster the nerve to try, my tongue crawls to the back of my throat, rendering me unable to talk and causing me to start sneezing profusely! Go figure.

Lacking the distraction that comes with dating however, I'm better able to prioritize my studies to get ready for senior year and beyond. To that end, one of my teachers, as well as the school counselor, recommends that I take an AP (Advance Placement) course and join a club called the Future Business Leaders of America (FBLA). Members of FBLA get to leave school early to go to a job. You simply report the hours you work for school credit.

I like the idea, so that's what I do. I leave school every day at noon to work at a Chuck E. Cheese. These family restaurants-slash-indoor kids' carnival are awash in bright colors and noises and kids having birthday parties. There's also the famous stage with a band of mechanical animals playing the Chuck E. Cheese theme song every twenty minutes. I guess these are dues you pay to belong to the FBLA!

Chuck E. Cheese is good to me, though. I even save up enough money over the summer after my junior year to buy my first car – a 1983 white Honda Prelude. *Is there anything to match your first car!*

Toward the end of my senior year, we are encouraged to put some kind of plan in place for what to do next – whether college, the military, or work. During Military Week at school, one of my friends decides he wants to join the Army. And I want to join the Air Force so I can learn to fly.

"That sounds great! Let's go sign up," I say.

I'm already imagining what life in the military will be like – all the traveling and training and comradery. I'm thinking of how exciting it will be to learn to fly a fighter jet or perhaps a chopper.

My imagining is abruptly interrupted by the recruiter however, when he says to me, "Son, with your eyesight your chances of flying are slim to none. Pilots are required to have 20/20 vision."

My dream of becoming a military pilot crashes and burns before it ever gets off the ground. I walk away from the recruiting table with my tail between my legs and my hope of learning to fly in the rearview mirror.

The next week I meet with the school guidance counselor to talk to her about my plans after high school. I tell her what I wanted, which was to fly in the Air Force, but explain that this option is off the table. As for college, I figure I can't afford it.

Her recommendation is that I take this test called the "SAT" which costs about $150. In my mind, spending that kind of money on a test sounds *crazy*. Since starting school, I've been taking tests *for free!* But I take her advice and pay the $150 and sit for the test.

Unfortunately, I do not score well. And I certainly don't plan to pay another $150 to take it again. But the counselor says she should be able to get me on a HOPE scholarship, as long as I maintain a 3.0 or higher grade point average until graduation.

"Go ahead and sign up now. If you don't get approved, you don't have to go. But if you do, you're already a step ahead."

That makes sense to me, so I sign up. I have my eye on Dekalb College. It's close enough and has a solid reputation for being a great school. What's funny is the more I think about it, the more I really want to go to college.

After graduating high school, I utilize a recruiting firm called Randstad to apply for a job at Ciba Vision. Ciba Vision is a large corporation in Atlanta that manufactures contact lenses. I know they hire a lot of students, so I figure my chance of getting hired there is pretty good. Besides, it's too early to register for college, and I need the money. When I walk in, one of the girls recognizes me: "I know you!"

"From where?"

"Don't you remember me? You worked at Chuck E. Cheese. I had a birthday party for my son a couple of weeks ago, and you were the one that took care of us!"

"Ahhhh… that's right."

A week later she calls and tells me that I got the job at Ciba.

It doesn't pay much – $5.10 per hour, in fact. But if everything goes well, after three months I could become permanent, and my payrate would go up to $9.00 an hour. Three months goes by fast and sure enough, before I know it, I'm making 9 bucks an hour… with benefits!

But now it's time to register for college. And my challenge is to figure out how to pay for the tuition that isn't covered by the HOPE scholarship. I get some help in the form of a student loan and put the rest on a credit card.

And then a few days before classes start, I tell my boss I'll have to quit because I'm starting school. He doesn't want me to quit because I'm a dependable employee. So he suggests I work on weekends only, and let Ciba help pay for my college. If my grades warrant it, he says, Ciba will reimburse my tuition!

To make this happen, I have to work twelve-hour shifts Saturdays and Sundays, but I get a 15-percent shift differential for working weekends which is pretty good for an 18-year-old. So that's what I do.

And in addition to paying for school, I'm able to save up enough to buy my first big-ticket item: a brand-new Honda Prelude "Sports Edition." *Hog heaven!* (That's an expression I learned early on, living in the South.)

My Prelude has an isobaric speaker that takes up the whole trunk, and through which I blast Dr. Dre and Snoop Dogg, with the dropping bass. You guessed it. I like my music loud!

In addition to my new ride, it's time I rethink my living situation, now that Sidan and his wife have two-year-old twin boys. When I'm not working or in class, I hang out at *Waffle House* or *Denny's* to study – not because Sidan's house is too noisy. I just don't want to be in the way.

Then a thought hits me. Mom and Dad now live in the heart of Atlanta. What if…

So I make a phone call, and here's how that conversation with Mom goes:

"Hi Mom… I'm moving in."

"Sideth! I'm so glad!"

And that was that – once again they welcome me with open arms.

It's early 1995. I'm a sophomore at Georgia State University now, still working at Ciba Vision, with a brand-spanking new car… and no girlfriend.

One of the more curious things to me is how friends move in and out of your life, and then back in again. Seems like I experience that more than most people, and it's about to happen again.

Peter (now a senior at Georgia Tech), JJ, and I start hanging out a lot more. As a result, in no time we become as close as we were as kids.

Not only that, we develop certain rituals. For example, every Tuesday evening we go to Dottie's Bar, play a little pool and drink a little cheap beer. How long we stay and where we go next all depends on our mood and the situation.

Sometimes we climb the Coca-Cola billboard. Yep. We do that. So I know it can be done… though I cannot recommend it! And at other times we settle on some other bar – Maggie's, Phoenix, occasionally The Masquerade, or whatever happens to be open and close by.

But without fail, once 2:00 a.m. rolls around you'll find us at the Clermont Lounge. Now, I won't try to describe this place to you, and neither will anyone else who's ever been there probably. But it is a crazy cool place.

In fact, this next story happens at the Clermont Lounge. But before sharing it, let me take a moment to say that when you dodge bullets and run for dear life at the tender age of six… eat whatever rodents and bugs your older brother can forage for you… and watch several of your siblings die of starvation right in front of you… you can truly appreciate the good life, especially the little, senseless things.

So what I hope you take away from this next story is that there is hope beyond despair. Life can be enjoyed, no matter what you may have been through. Good, simple fun can come back into your life. I know that because if you saw me now you would never guess I had suffered so much loss as a child.

The Clermont is a hotel. But let's just say you would not be renting a room here if you were looking for a good night's sleep.

Like a lot of hotels, Clermont has a lounge. But their lounge is in the basement. And they must have acquired a special-privilege liquor license or something because they are able to sell beer after 2:00 a.m. (Now you know why we are here after two o'clock in the morning!)

This place is kind of a shrine, in a way. It's an old Atlanta institution that I can best describe as a retro/hip/funk/strip club kind of scene. It attracts all sorts of people. And famous musicians often just show up here for fun, unexpected and unrehearsed, and do a show. Or sometimes they just chill with everybody else.

One very late Tuesday night (Wednesday morning technically), Peter,

JJ, and I go to the Clermont. We find some seats, order some beers, and sit back to enjoy the spectacle.

The next thing we know local Atlanta celebrity *Blondie* (full *nom de guerre* Blondie Strange) shows up to entertain us!

I can't believe what I'm seeing. Blondie, well known in Atlanta for a certain, uhhh… *talent* which she is about to demonstrate, saunters over to the bar wearing nothing but a bikini.

She gets an empty beer can from a patron and proceeds to put it between her breasts. And then with one seamless movement she squeezes her boobs with her hands, crushing the beer can. When she removes it from the site of destruction, it's as flat as if you'd stomped it as hard as you could on a concrete floor with a size 15 shoe!

The place bursts into applause. I'm amazed, confused, dumbfounded, excited – *what just happened?*

I pull out a $20 bill.

"I want to see this up close to make sure it's not some fake trick or something."

Blondie walks right up to me.

Holy Mary, what's about to happen?!

And I, somewhat emboldened by alcohol, ask her: "Is that for real? Can I see that again?"

She obliges me, taking my half-finished beer, pouring it out, and again, *crunch!* That can is as flat as if a Mack truck had run over it. Move over, David Copperfield – we got this!

But the magic doesn't stop here.

Remember I said I'd like to see that right in front of me? Well, as I'm standing there dumbfounded, Blondie grabs me by the back of my head with her two hands and pulls my face down between her boobs.

While wondering for one blinding moment if she's about to flatten my face like a beer can… I go black.

Yep, I pass out!

And when I come to, the first thing I see is Peter and JJ rolling in the floor, laughing their asses off.

I have no idea what just happened! My lips are a little salty and a bit numb. I touch the numb part of my mouth and come away with blood on my fingers.

Blondie just busted my lips with her boobs – *what a crazy night!!!*

Believe it or not, Peter, JJ, and I haven't quite had enough. It's now about 4:00 a.m., and we leave Clermont and take off walking down Ponce de Leon Avenue. Up the road we see a flashing marquee on one of the buildings. The neon sign says *Phoenix Cocktail Lounge*.

"Hmmm… okay, let's try this place," says Peter. The first thing I notice as we walk in is that there are no females. Okay, well maybe the lucky guys got hooked up with all the girls that were here and went back home.

But somehow the guys here look a little different. Most of them are wearing tight leather pants. Some even have dog collars with spikes around their necks. Most are pretty well built. In fact, they look a lot like bikers, except there are no bikes parked out front. Oh, well…

We sit down at the bar. I'm at the end, Peter's in the middle, and JJ is what you might call first in line. We order our beer. I'm scoping the place to see if there are, in fact, any females that I might have missed at first glance. Nada.

With our beer half drunk, one of the guys comes up to JJ and says something. Nothing bad, as it turns out, just an expression of appreciation… of sorts. Immediately JJ jumps up and says emphatically, *"IT'S TIME TO GO!"*

Another notable adventure involves one of my good friends who went to Emory. This guy is brilliant, if a bit crazy – in a good way. For instance, he once jumped out of the car at a red light at 2:00 in the morning to moon everyone passing by. The cars that drive by honk in concert. Me… I was in our car laughing my tail off. It was so ridiculous. This guy didn't have a care or worry bone in his body!

He once gave me a picture in a frame for my birthday. The picture was this black-and-white image of a man looking at a brick wall, and on the wall is the face of a beautiful woman. Leaning against the bottom of the wall is a simple bike. And on the left-hand side there's a dirt road.

Instantly this picture brings a scene to my mind. I see Père, my foster father, stopping for a brief respite while returning home on his bike down a dirt road. The face of the beautiful woman? That's my real mom, thanking him for risking his life to save mine.

I'm glad that picture makes me think of Père… and my mom.

All the people, events, and situations in our lives are pieces in a puzzle – a grand design that indicates a Higher Intelligence is at work. This Being – someone much bigger than ourselves – is showing us something that, at the time, we likely miss. It's only much later that we realize a significant occurrence has happened. Providence has been at work all along.

Surprisingly, I'm not sure I would have ever paused and reflected enough on the entirety of my life to recognize all those people and events and situations that God brought me to and through had I not made the decision to write this book. The situation I'm about to share with you will demonstrate what I mean.

I'm working the weekend shift at Ciba Vision around 1995 or 1996. Usually at breaktime we all go to a pavilion area at the back of our building. But this particular evening I decide to take my break at the front of the building. I'm not really in the mood to socialize, as I seem to have a lot on my mind for some reason. I just want to be alone to think.

The sun is low in the sky, but there is still plenty of daylight. I find a place to sit and just look at the sky. The sky has always fascinated me – whether day or night – and gazing at its beauty never fails to make me feel at peace.

While lost in my daydreams, out of nowhere a man walks up to me. I don't recognize him… and yet I do. He's a familiar figure from another time and place, like someone lost in my memory that I haven't seen or thought about in a very long time.

And then it hits me.

"Hi…" I say, slowly. "Are you Jerry Percifield?" He looks puzzled for an instant, and then his eyes get brighter and his face lights up all over.

"Yes, I am! *And you're Sideth!*"

"Yes, sir."

I'm more than a little surprised, caught off guard and a bit tongue-tied all at once. I have no idea what to say.

But Jerry takes the lead on our conversation, asking me why I am sitting in front of this office. I tell him, of course.

As Providence would have it, Jerry, an architect by trade, has just won the bid on an expansion project for Ciba. Consequently, he needed to make a trip here today to come and check out our buildings.

We only chat for a bit. But that is long enough for me to share with him just how his magnanimous goodness and efforts on my behalf have changed my life. I tell him this is equally true for the rest of my family he rescued. And I am sure to ask him to please pass my words on to his wife, Libby. For she was an equal partner in the goodness shown us.

In a few short minutes we part ways again. I'm on the clock and have to get back to work.

So in the blink of an eye, Jerry's gone. Gone… but as the saying goes, *certainly* not forgotten.

Peter has now graduated from Georgia Tech and is working for an engineering company that requires he travel a lot. About this same time, JJ moves… which means my social life is having to adjust. But I'm still in college and not ready to quit having fun just yet.

So another student at Georgia State and I start hanging out when we have time to spare, though his own group of friends keeps him busy most of the time. And I'm glad that's the case, because I need to focus on school anyway.

But when we do have time, everybody congregates at his place. It's an active bunch, so we do our share of camping, hiking, whitewater rafting, rock climbing, and repelling together.

Through this guy I also meet Victor, who lives in Florida. Victor happens to be visiting his friend one weekend, and he and I really hit it off. In fact, when he moves to Georgia about a year later (after getting married), we become best friends.

It seems like I'm all over the place my senior year. In addition to being a full-time college student, my job consumes my weekends. And I've even taken on some additional responsibilities at work that involve coming into the office one day during the week. I'm now considered both a full-time student *and* a full-time employee.

But somehow, I manage to find time to hang out with these guys. And somewhere else I also find time for a hobby.

"How would you like to learn to play golf?" my boss asks me one day.

I don't know how to answer that question, because I've never had a chance to give golf a try.

Given I need some help making that decision, my boss starts explaining how the game works. And there is something in particular in his explanation that catches my attention...

"If you join the golf league," he says, "you'll meet a lot of people who can help you with your career when you graduate."

That's all I need to know.

And as it turns out, I'm actually a natural golfer. I even end up winning four trophies over the next year or so. And in the process, I meet one of the managers at Ciba, an engineer named Armando.

Then it's August 1998 – a very special date for me. After taking five years to do it – with some help from student loans, tuition reimbursement, a credit card, and living with Mom and Dad – I graduate from Georgia State with a BBA. It is my greatest accomplishment to date, at least in my mind.

I want Mom to share her words with you about this:

> I did not cry when my daughter, Sarah, graduated from Emory. I did not cry when my son, Peter, graduated from Georgia Tech. But when I saw Sideth walking down the aisle to get his diploma from Georgia State, I cried like a baby.
>
> In an instant I saw that little fella that was brought into my classroom one morning. He was dressed in pants and a shirt that were both ragged and outgrown... and an old pair of adult tennis shoes tied on his feet.
>
> I remember him looking up at me and saying, *"No Mama. No Papa."*
>
> I saw the joy in his eyes when we walked out of the mall that Friday afternoon after being outfitted in a new pair of green Nike tennis shoes that were just his size. I'm sure that in his mind he believed they had been made just for him.
>
> I saw the radiance in his face while enjoying weekends and holidays with our family, and how much he loved visiting Nanny and Papa. I recall how proud he was when he got a job... and bought a car... and enrolled in college.
>
> All those visits and adventures and dinners together watching him slowly grow to become the man he is today came back to me all at once.
>
> The blessing he has been to me personally and professionally, the joy he has brought our family, the honor and pride I feel every time he calls me "Mom," causes my heart to overflow. Words cannot describe what Sideth means to me... what he will *always* mean to me.

22

Gaining and Losing

Now that I've graduated college, I hardly know what to do with myself. Going from full-time student and full-time employee to just full-time employee has cut my workload in half overnight. Another bonus is that a Monday-through-Friday workweek also frees up my weekends!

Within a couple weeks after assuming this new schedule, I get a visit from Armando, one of Ciba's managers I met through the golf league. He offers me a job in his department. I decide to accept because Armando and I are great friends. And it doesn't hurt that this position comes with a little bump in pay!

Not long after settling in, the thought hits me one day out of the blue that I want to become a U.S. citizen. You may wonder why I haven't considered this before. The reason is probably because none of my Cambodian family has yet pursued citizenship.

To be honest, I think I want to be an American, but I have no idea what the practical benefit of this would be. Certainly, the first thing that comes to mind is the right to vote. But at this time in my life I don't care about voting. I'm sure you understand why I say I hate politics. (Not surprisingly, it is the only college class I ever got an "F" in.)

But now that I have a job and a car... and at least one American family... it seems like the thing to do. How hard can it be, after all?

I take the test. It consists of ten questions, that's all. And lo and behold, I fail it. (Frankly, I'm not sure most Americans could pass it.)

The lady is nice, though. "Sorry, Sideth. You'll have to retake the test – but this should help you. Here are the questions you missed, and here's a study guide to help you with the answers."

I take the next three months to devour the study guide which consists of a thousand questions about U.S. history. But it pays off. This time around I pass. In fact, now that it's done, I'm actually glad I failed the test the first time. I now know a lot more about U.S. history than the average natural-born American citizen walking the street.

Besides, failure doesn't really bother me. The way I see it, failure is the main ingredient to success. Failure also helps you truly appreciate the sweet taste of success when it does come your way.

But what means more to me than passing the test and gaining U.S. citizenship is the love and support I receive for doing it. Mom and Dad, Nanny and Papa all come to see me get sworn in. How proud I am to make them proud of me... and happy for me!

And to top it off, the next day when I get to work, I am greeted with a *"WELCOME TO AMERICA"* party, compliments of Armando. The party has an *"American Pie"* theme that includes the legendary song by Don McClean, a pie with a flag design on it and, of course, American flags everywhere! I'll never forget that day.

It's 1999, and the notable event this year is a wedding. Peter marries Chrissy, the love of his life. Thankfully, Chrissy and I get along well, so she's good with my tagging along.

So Peter is married now. And I...

Well, I'm still living with Mom and Dad. It's no disgrace, I know. But it weighs on me.

Then one day I happen to run into Victor, the guy from Florida that I met through a mutual friend. In the process of catching up, he tells me that since we last saw each other he got married... and divorced. Not only that, he's currently unemployed and has moved back in with his parents.

It takes me a minute or two to get my head around all this.

"You doing okay, man? That's a lot of major life changes in that length of time."

"Oh yeah. I had a tough time getting through some of it, but I'm okay now."

Once I get my bearings, I realize we still have something in common. I know how it feels to be living with your parents. In the process of our conversation I tell him how I want to get out on my own and really do something different.

That must have been just what Victor wanted to hear. "Hey, how about we rent an apartment together? The only problem is that without a job I'm shy on cash. But we can live with my mom and dad right now and then get a place as soon as I get a job."

(I know Victor's mom and dad, having spent a lot of time at their house when we first met. They are a couple of angels, and another of those couples who love me like their own son.)

"Besides, it's really close to where you work."

He did have a point there. So I move out of Mom and Dad's and in with Victor's family. One month turns into two, and then three. And the next thing I know, it's the next spring, and Victor and I are still living with his parents.

I seem to have this pattern of being adopted. It started in Cambodia with my Mère and Père. Then it was Aunt Sim. Then the Hughes' family. And now Victor's family!

They have welcomed me into their home with as much love as any other *adoptive* family I've known. We go on trips together. We go camping and whitewater rafting together. The four of us even take a trip to Germany together!

But as amazing as life is for me right now, I'm antsy. I am ready to be an independent soul… out in the world, on my own.

So while Victor and I are grilling out one evening (Victor's a really great cook in addition to being a brilliant guy), I feel the need to ask him, "So, what's the next big adventure?"

"I don't know. But I'll be on my feet again soon," he says.

I wanted so bad to say… "Yeah, but you're still living with your parents. *We're* still living with your parents. We need to make a change bro', now!" But instead I keep that to myself.

Rather, I offer the following…

I know this guy, he's a friend of mine – an old boss I used to work for actually. Between my referral and your ability to present yourself, he'll probably hire you on the spot. You'll just have to learn how to use this tool that makes contact lenses. But hey, if I can do it, you sure can. It may not be your dream job, but it'll get you out of the house and back on your feet.

I'm thinking... *Victor is a 4.0 GPA aviation school graduate. How hard can this be?*

Victor gets the job at Ciba, like I thought he would. But we still don't get around to moving out. His parents are beyond kind and understanding. They never put pressure on us to move out. Of course, now that we work most of the time and go out most nights, we rarely cross paths with them anyway.

After Victor has been at Ciba a few months, I move from the administrative building to the manufacturing facility. Now we're in the same building.

Our company happens to be hiring a lot of military personnel. Before you know it, we have a group of six or seven friends from work, several of whom are ex-military.

This is one of the best times of my life. Our working atmosphere is like a college campus. And not only that, Ciba offers an after-work program that a lot of us take advantage of. I play golf and volleyball. Victor plays softball. Some of the guys are involved in all three. It is an awesome work-play environment.

Sometime in the middle of the summer that year one of our friends drops by after work to see if we want to go clubbing at this place in Buckhead. I've been there many times, and it's a mob scene. Besides, I'm beat. All I really want to do right now is kick back, have a drink, and listen to some music.

But Victor would have none of it. "Come on, none of us works tomorrow. It's the perfect time to go out... *and we certainly don't want to disappoint the girls, now do we?*"

He's getting on my nerves, but it is clear I am the only party pooper, so I give in. "Okay, but I'll be the DD [designated driver]."

On the way to Buckhead, the guy that got this all started *just happens* to mention that one of the girls we're headed to meet is interested in Victor. And it turns out the other one is interested in another of our friends.

I understand now. This is a date setup. *And here again I am the fifth wheel.* Now, I know these girls; a couple of them have just recently moved down from New York City. But we don't hang out together, so none of us knows them very well.

Thanks to the never-ending parking problem that is Atlanta, there are no available spots when we get to the club. So I park at a nearby Publix supermarket to avoid having to pay.

Once we get inside, there's a lot going on. Most of the patrons are dancing. But out of the corner of my eye I notice one of the two girls – her name is Christina – sitting at the bar, drinking alone.

Now, I was raised by gentle people to be a gentleman, and I don't want her to feel left out. So, I go over and put my arm around her and say hello.

Okay, maybe that was a bit forward. But my intentions are good – and I feel comfortable doing it because we are friends. Under these circumstances I figure I can even ask her if she'd like to dance. So I do.

What happens next takes me completely off guard.

She leans away and squinches her face into this look of total revulsion. She even said a few choice words, I think. I'm kind of thankful I can't hear her for all the noise. I don't need to, however. That look says it all.

With that, I turn and start toward the door. On the way, I convince some of the other guys to leave here and go to a club called Havana. The rest of our party heads in some other direction.

Since everything shuts down at 2:00 a.m. as far as clubbing is concerned (except for the Clermont Lounge!), we eventually all meet back at the Publix parking lot.

When we get there, we discover immediately that Victor's car has been *booted*. Some jerk put a lock on one of the wheels so the car can't be driven.

We are furious. *After all, we parked in a publix lot! (pun intended).* And it is obvious Publix isn't running out of spaces. But ranting does no good. We have to pay the piper - *seventy* bucks to get that boot removed!

Believe it or not, sometime after the uncomfortable encounter between Christina and me at the bar that night, we start warming up to each other.

And I find that once I get to know her, she's alright. She must have decided I wasn't so bad either, because we are becoming really good friends.

And then a few months into our friendship, I start getting this feeling that she's interested in me. To be honest, I'm kind of shell-shocked, considering that infamous night. Nevertheless, we start dating… in a platonic sort of way. A few weeks later, Christina and I become an official couple!

Not long after this, another stride forward happens. Victor and I finally get an apartment together and move out of his parents' house. I also make the decision to change careers. I leave Ciba for a promising position as a business analyst with a company called Paragon Trade Brand.

Life rocks on and everything is going great. Then that summer I decide to take a little time off to make the trip to Canada to visit Sovannary. On my way home I get a call from Peter.

"Papa's gone."

No. I lose my breath. I can't believe it. And then it dawns on me that I haven't felt this feeling of horrible emptiness that comes with losing a family member since I was a kid in Cambodia. It hurts terribly, and the pain is compounded by all the ghosts of my past.

I find out later that not long before Papa passed, he requested that his grandsons be his pallbearers. And he specifically told Mom, who was with him at the time, to be sure and include me in that group. There are no words to express how blessed and honored that makes me feel.

The day of his funeral I realize that all the dying I saw firsthand when I was a lot younger left me unable to manage death… and funerals… well at all. I am *devastated* by his loss.

With his casket on my shoulder, all those wonderful memories I have with Papa flood my mind. I remember a time when I barely spoke English but still knew his favorite word was *"yonder."* I remember him taking us alligator hunting and chasing us with his cane and telling us to dig holes just to fill them up again.

I sure miss all that right now. I miss Papa. The hole that is now left in my heart by his passing will never be filled.

Life moves on. It's now 2002, and with my new job I realize I have enough income to buy a house. So instead of signing another year lease with Victor, I decide to take the plunge and become a homeowner.

Victor rents a house across the street from his parents which I honestly think is a good idea. He hasn't been the same since his divorce, and he needs to be close to his family.

But only a couple months after signing papers on my mortgage, my company gets bought out by Tyco Healthcare and moves the headquarters to King of Prussia, Pennsylvania.

Isn't it funny how life works? Now I have a decision to make. I can stay with the company and move to King of Prussia… or take six months' severance pay and say goodbye.

You can probably guess what I do. I have just bought a house, after all. But now I have a mortgage to pay and no job. And an ulcer that I can tell is getting worse. I don't let anybody know, though. I decide to just keep it to myself and ride it out.

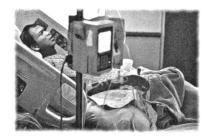

23

Almost Gone... Again

Summer days in the South see the thermometer climb above the 90-degree mark with no trouble. Add in the equivalent percentage of humidity, and you get our forecast for today – hot and humid.

Despite the weather however, I told Victor that I'd help him put an engine in a boat he recently bought. And after that, we're going to paint it.

But I wake up feeling a little dizzy and feverish, with a twinge of pain in my right side. It's like a tiny knife is carving on my insides. I can tell that what I had for breakfast is trying to come back up... and does.

But now that that's done, I decide I'm good to go. Besides, I promised Victor I'd help, and I'm sticking to my promise.

His boat is docked at Lake Lanier, so we're planning to just meet up there. Christina decides she's going with me, which is a good thing because the way I feel this morning I don't think I should be driving.

When we walk outside to get in the car, everything seems brighter than usual... but not in a fun, *gee-what-a-nice-sunny-day* kind of way. The sunlight is piercing – and painful.

What's even more curious is the fact that I'm downright cold. The thermometer is already ticking in the mid 80's, but I am cold.

On the way there, my stomach hurts so bad that I ask Christina to pull into a McDonald's so I can relieve myself. My stool is as black as charcoal.

I'm sweating profusely and my stomach hurts terribly, even worse than before we left.

Christina gets me a sandwich while waiting for me, but I can't stand the thought of eating.

By the time we catch up with Victor, he has already put the motor in. It's time to clean and paint, so I grab a rag and start cleaning the front left side of the boat.

About an hour in I'm feeling so awful that I say, *"I think I'll just call the Khmer Rouge over to finish me off."*

"You're white as a sheet, man."

"Well, you're pretty white yourself," I say, trying to sound the part.

"He's still got his sense of humor," Victor says, winking and glancing in Christina's direction.

Then they start some version of back-and-forth about whether I should go to the hospital. I let them know immediately that option is off the table. In the end, they both agree that at the very least, Christina needs to get me home.

We are back in the car. I'm pouring sweat... and at the same time I'm so cold I can't stop shivering. I'm also incredibly dizzy. And if all that's not bad enough, I'm about to lose my lunch, even though I didn't have any.

As soon as Christina pulls into the driveway, I open the door and fall to the ground on my knees. Instantly up comes something that looks like part of an intestine covered in blood... *lots of blood!* It's all over the grass in front of me.

Somehow Christina helps me up to my room, though I can't remember how we get there. I'm now drifting in and out of consciousness. She spends the next hour or so begging me to go to the emergency room, but I persistently refuse.

I hate hospitals. My natural mom died in a hospital. How and why her life ended I never knew. I never wanted to know.

But ever since, every time I'm in a hospital I can smell death. And immediately I'm back in that hospital in Cambodia hoping to visit my mom – a visit that never took place.

Besides, if past trauma isn't reason enough – I'm also between jobs right now and have no insurance. Hospital care is expensive, and I don't have the money to pay for it.

But Christina won't let it go. So I finally compromise. I tell her she can call Sarah, Peter's sister, who is a nurse. "If Sarah says I need to go, I'll go."

"Good," Christina breathes a sigh of relief. I think I notice tears in her eyes.

"But be sure and tell her I feel fine now," I say. "I'm just sleepy."

After several unsuccessful attempts to reach Sarah, Christina opts to call the nurse hotline from the back of her insurance card instead. Once she explains everything, the nurse tells her she must get me to the hospital immediately as my situation is critical. And since I promised I'd be willing to go if necessary, I really have no choice. I have to go.

My memory of how we get from my house to the emergency room is a little on the blank side, however. I must have gotten worse, and somehow Christina managed the situation. That's all I know.

The next thing I remember is trying to explain to the triage nurse how I feel. I don't think I'm making sense. Then a wheelchair appears out of nowhere. For someone not staring death in the face (at least that's what I think), this is the fastest service I have ever seen in a hospital. They put tubes up my nose and down my throat like they're trying to break some kind of record.

The pain is coming back, and I am not in a nice mood. I decide that I hate everything and everybody. I'm so angry about being in the hospital that I start yelling at Christina, who's just sitting there. She's done nothing this whole time but be right by my side, and I'm hurling abuse at her. But to be fair, I hardly even know what I'm doing.

I tell her to go home; I don't want her to see me like this. Everything is irritating me. I don't know if it's the effect of some of the medicine they've given me or what. I've never been so irritated before – at least not since getting to America.

Christina is a trooper though. She doesn't go anywhere. This just irritates me even more. I feel vulnerable. Exposed.

I make her promise not to tell any of my family about any of this. I don't want them worrying about me. "This whole thing…" I say, trying to convince myself, "it'll pass. It always does."

Another item in the long list of what's irritating me is that we appear to be in some emergency room holding pattern. Now that they've plugged me into everything imaginable, I think they actually forget we're here. Whatever they plan to do, they're certainly taking long enough to do it.

I'm sure that at least an hour passes before they check my blood, and it's another hour before the nurse comes back in.

"I have some bad news," she says.

We wait.

"You have to be admitted."

"Oh, hell, no. No way."

She continues as if she doesn't hear me. "Your blood count is extremely low. It has to be at a certain level before I can release you."

"And when will that happen?"

"Well," she says slowly, "I don't know how long it will take. I only know that for the time being, we cannot let you go."

I am so angry I could pick up a chair and throw it through the window – or at somebody… although my ability to actually do so is definitely in question.

With Christina's help, I manage to calm down a bit. To my dismay, they wheel me to a private room. And then every hour they proceed to poke me with a needle. Along with hospitals, I *hate* needles!

Needles. Needles and snakes are my two phobias. And here I am in a hospital surrounded by needles. That makes about as much sense as climbing to the top of the Empire State Building if you're afraid of heights.

I make it through that night though – a miracle in itself. But now that it's the next day, I'm ready to go home and get this behind me.

"Nope," says the nurse. "That's not going to happen. You lost so much blood that we have to keep giving you more until your level is back to normal."

I am furious with that news. But my anger and protestations don't faze her. She turns and leaves the room as if I had said nothing.

"Okay," I tell myself. "I'll lie here for a little while longer."

I stare at this tube in my arm for what feels like hours. But at some point, I've had all I can stand. I call the nurse and demand to be released.

Two nurses come to my room. And when I repeat my demands, they actually look at each other and laugh. *"Sorry, fella. You're not going any-where just yet."*

Since my threats are not enough to convince them, I talk myself into just sitting tight and picking this up again tomorrow.

But the next morning, before I can implement my plan, two nurses come in and promptly proceed to transfer me to a mobile bed and wheel me toward another room. While being pushed down the hall, a doctor joins us to ask a few questions. And then he says, "Okay, I'm going to fix up your stomach. You have some persistent bacteria that requires an operation."

I understand now… the *operating room* is our destination – this really big, cold room with a lot of bright lights and machines.

Once we get there, a flurry of activity starts that I have no idea about. The nurse puts a tube with some kind of gas coming out of it under my nose.

"Okay," the anesthesiologist says, "I want you to count from ten backward to zero."

"Ten, nine…"

In that instant before going out, flashing across my mind is a memory of another time in my life when someone transported me on a set of wheels in an attempt to save my life.

Immediately another image replaces that one. I see a blazing red evening sky and a lot of leaves – maybe a jungle – and people in masks with knives making a circle around me.

The next thing I remember, I'm back in my room. And Christina, faithful as always, is right there.

I am convinced that I'm ready to go home. But it's night, the best I can tell (believe it or not, this room has no windows). And having heard nothing about when I will be discharged, I call for the nurse.

"Can I go home now?" I ask.

"Once the doctor releases you, I'll be happy to let you go. But as of now, he hasn't." She continues, "He will be in first thing in the morning to give you an update. Until then, just try to relax and rest… you've been through quite an ordeal!"

Reluctantly I agree. But I'm not happy about it.

In a few more hours there's another shift change, which means another nurse comes in and starts my needle-sticking routine for the day. (Surprisingly, I'm almost used to it by now.)

Suddenly, the nurse's eyes get wide. I'm thinking… "Oh no, what now?"

"Sideth!" She wasn't just reading my name; she said it like she knew me and was surprised to see me.

"Sideth – what are you doing here?"

My first thought is, "Where the heck do I begin?"

"Do you remember me?" she asks.

I hadn't really noticed her, thinking she was just another one of my nurses. But when she says that, and I take a better look at her face, I certainly do remember her!

She's from Nigeria. For the life of me I cannot remember her name, but back in 1996 we both worked for Ciba Vision. I was head of her department and the technician overseeing her work. We were both students at the time, working those long Saturday/Sunday shifts.

"So what's going on with you?" she asks while drawing my blood.

"I was laid off…"

"No – I mean, what are you doing *here?*"

"Well… why not here?"

She looks at me like I'm from another world, and I think I hear her say, "You're in *Camp Seven.*"

"What?"

"I said, you're on Floor Number Seven."

"Oh." I'm obviously disoriented. It takes me a minute, but eventually I just start laughing. "Okay. So what about it? What's wrong with 'Floor Seven?'"

She gives me this serious look, as if she's trying to wake me up. *"Sideth… this is the floor where people come to die."* Then she freezes, as if realizing she just said something she shouldn't have.

But now I understand why she is so surprised. She probably figures I know all about the Seventh Floor, and how critical my situation is.

"But I feel fine," I explain. "I'm not gonna die." I try to sound confident, *though I'm not exactly sure if I should be now!*

"Well," she says gently, putting her hand on my shoulder, "this is my first day back from vacation, so let me see what's going on…"

She walks out and is gone long enough for me to wonder what just happened and to seriously consider why I *AM* here. All the while in the back of my mind I continue to remind myself that I am fine. I am fine. *I am fine?*

Then she returns. "Well, you lost a lot of blood. They had to put somewhere between three and four pints back in you. And they have to make sure everything's stable before letting you go."

"But what is *wrong* with me?"

She starts telling me, but I can't focus on what she's saying because the realization of what she just told me about the Seventh Floor starts sinking in.

She stops talking, and then leaves the room again. I get up, thinking *"I've got to get out of here."*

So I get out of bed and start walking down the hall… when I'm hit with that smell again. That damn smell. *That death smell.* Once you experience that smell, it never leaves you. I thought I'd forgotten all about it. I guess one can't be so lucky.

I feel a hand firmly grip my bicep. I look around to see another nurse. After some effort, she's able to talk me off the cliff by convincing me that being on this floor doesn't necessarily mean anything now. All my readings look stable, and since I'm feeling good, I should be able to go home soon.

I don't know how much of this is true and how much of it is just her getting control of the situation, but I go with it. She wins… and I go back to my room.

The next morning the doctor comes in and briefs me on my condition.

"Sideth," he says, "you lost a lot of blood. We had to stabilize you by giving you blood transfusions. And then once your levels stabilized, we had to operate. You had a very bad ulcer that was inflamed. The only way we could stop the bleeding was to operate. But you should be all fixed up now."

While continuing to talk, he pulls a chair close to my bed, sits down and takes some time to look over my chart.

Here it comes, I thought. And immediately I'm six again, on that dirt road with Père when the Khmer Rouge are about to kill us. And in my mind, I hear Père begging them… *"please don't kill us, please don't, please don't."*

I'm saying the same thing now in my head. "Just let it be quick. At least I can rest then. At least there will be no more worrying."

"Sideth," the doctor says, trying to pull me back to the present. "If you had gotten here an hour later, you would've most likely had a cardiac arrest. You probably would have died from the internal bleeding."

He stands up. "But thankfully, you seem to be recovering well after the surgery. We have to get a couple more samples, and if all that looks okay, you will be good to go, sir!"

Some months later I am struck with two realizations from this experience. First, here is yet another instance of Providence watching out for me. (I've lost count of how many near-death experiences I have lived through.)

I honestly don't think I would still be here had Christina not been with me… and if she had not insisted that I go to the hospital. I foolishly stood my ground and resisted her for most of that day. *If the doctor was right, one more hour would have done me in.*

Second, if you recall, I was between jobs when this happened. And between jobs translates to being between insurance coverages. That was another reason I was so insistent that I not go to the hospital in the first place. I had no idea how I would pay for it.

I dread going to the mailbox for a few weeks after being back home. I can only imagine what kind of astronomical figure I will be owing that hospital. A three-day hospital stay that included major surgery will cost me tens of thousands.

But I never got a bill! *I never even got the first piece of mail* about owing anybody – doctor *or* hospital.

All I can figure is that the hospital waived the charges (but why would they do that?) or someone paid my bill for me. All I know is this – the hospitalization, the surgery – I was never charged a penny.

184

24

On Success and Failure, Tragedy and Triumph

The three days I spent in the hospital with the bleeding ulcer – the experience that would've taken my life had it not been for Christina – was a definite turning point for me. Before then, at least in my mind, I was a refugee kid with no real purpose other than to continually be moving further away from my pain-riddled past.

I had now lived in America four times longer than I lived in my home country. Not only that, I was a legitimate American citizen. But I struggled to believe that I really belonged here.

Granted… I certainly didn't feel like I belonged in Cambodia either. *Lost* is the only word I have to describe how I felt.

I remember lying in that hospital bed with tubes coming out of my arms for what seemed like hours on end wishing I could just leave this world. But as much as I fought being there, that hospital experience led me to start asking those *big questions* like, *"Who am I,"* and *"What is my purpose for being here?"*

In short, those three days in that hospital room changed my life. While lying there, I was able to come up with some answers that work for me. Also, I was able to muster the motivation I needed to keep going.

I found purpose for my life. And I resolved to make a difference from that moment forward. I began thinking of my life in terms of four categories:

- Success
- Failure
- Tragedy
- Triumph

Because you've walked to this point in my journey with me, I'd like to share what I discovered with you.

Success

On October 29, 2006, Christina and I were married. If you remember back to that famous (or *infamous*) beginning at the club that night, I'd call that a rousing success!

Also, no matter how many times I've been laid off, I always managed to hold my own financially. Between 2008 and 2015, I worked for five different companies. You might say this was a hard patch – but again, not compared to Cambodia. After all I had been through there, I can survive this kind of thing blindfolded.

At one point during those seven years I was nearing the end of my proverbial rope when I found a contracting job at a technology company in Atlanta. That was the good news. The bad news was that it paid a fourth less than my previous salary. Thankfully I was able to adjust the budget and still manage to pay the mortgage and take care of my family's needs.

Besides being able to buy a house, I'm very proud of having paid for my own education. Graduating from Georgia State was my first major accomplishment. College was difficult... and scary. But I did it. And though it took me 16 years to pay off $50,000 of student loan debt, I did that too. I made my last payment November of 2014!

Another success I'm proud of is that through all this I learned the importance of saving. I'm pretty sure that if I died today, my wife and kids would be okay.

Because I have been given so much over the years, one of my primary goals in life is to give back. For that reason, the door of our home is always open to those in need of a place to stay. In fact, my friends refer to our home as *"Hotel Ung."*

Hotel Ung. I like that. It has a nice ring to it. And because it accomplishes one of my purposes in life, it goes in the success column.

But my greatest success, in my opinion, is our boys.

On June 16, 2008, Christina and I brought two beautiful twin boys into this world. At the time I hardly knew how to take care of myself, let alone two babies! It was like God was saying "Here you go… sink or swim!"

But we didn't just have twin boys, which would have been challenge enough. Our babies were three months premature! They weighed only three pounds each and had to stay at the hospital in incubators for over a month. We went to the hospital every day and helped the nurses care for our babies as best we could. Even when it was time to bring them home, they were still wired up to a machine that monitored almost everything that could be monitored.

In simple terms, I was scared to death. I had no idea how I would manage it all. My job was not close to home. The stress of fighting traffic, doing a good job at work as a new, sleep-deprived parent, then returning home to help my exhausted wife with our preemie twins… was more than enough challenge.

But as hard as that stretch was for Christina and me, our twin boys are a true gift – the kind of gift only parents understand.

Three years later, once life was relatively smooth and stable again, we had another son, Niko. Niko was born September 23, 2011, at seven-plus pounds and was healthy as could be.

Niko, by the way, is short for *Nikola*. We named him Nikola after Nikola Tesla, a renowned Croatian inventor and engineer you may have heard of. Christina is of Croatian descent, born in New York City to parents who were immigrants themselves. Niko's middle name is Sidan – in honor of my brother who is so dear to me.

At the point I became a father, I made a very conscious decision to live for my wife and kids and no longer for myself. Every decision I make is based on how it will affect and benefit them, and I can honestly say I'm very *intentional* about it.

For instance, I've given up golf completely. I never go to bars or play cards anymore. I'm not knocking those things, it's just that it's not for me at this point in my life.

And weekend *guy trips* with my buddies are also off the table. I had much rather spend my time with Christina taking in our boys' little league baseball games or taking them to the movies – complete with pop and popcorn, of course!

Failure

At the same time, I feel like one of my failures in life is not knowing how to raise our kids well. I'm too soft on them. I can't seem to put my foot down. I've tried, I really have. But that's not who I am. They know I love them; I make sure of that. But I'm just not good at *tough* love.

And then there's the problem with balancing work and home. In addition to required time at work, I spend about three hours a day just in traffic. By the time I get home I'm wiped out.

I want my boys involved in more sports at school that they want to participate in. I want to take them camping and hiking. I want to ride bikes, skateboard, and play kickball with them. But there just aren't enough hours in the day.

Not only does this make me feel like I'm failing as a father, this time crunch could mean that I may be failing as a husband as well.

All I know is that one of my priorities is to keep our family intact and give our kids a chance at a great life. And that includes a chance to grow up with a mom and dad and siblings… to know the stability and safety of a real family *for all their life.*

On a much different note, another of my failures has to do with climbing the corporate ladder. In short, I'm not very good at it.

I don't like playing the game, if you know what I mean. It's often political – people fighting people. Winners and losers.

That's just not my way. I may be oversimplifying the whole idea, but it has been called a *"rat race,"* after all. And, more often than not, that's what it feels like… at least to me. And for one who spent a good part of his early years subsisting on rat meat, I want nothing to do with *rats* of any kind!

While the chance to live in America and have a job that supports my family is an opportunity that I consider to be a true blessing, maybe the fact that I've been laid off so many times has something to do with the way I feel about it all. Nevertheless, I am grateful every day for the health to work and for a job to go to.

To sum up my failures, I'm not particularly rich, or highly educated, or even that great of a husband or parent. But after what I've been through, from my side of the fence most of what concerns me in these arenas is just small stuff. And I agree with whoever first said, "we shouldn't sweat the small stuff."

Tragedy

Everything that happened in Cambodia is certainly the worst tragedy I have experienced. But as horrible as that was – and it was *unspeakably* horrible – as a survivor I now truly appreciate the gift of life. For that reason, my definition of tragedy is *losing someone I love.*

The first person really close to me that I lost after coming to America was Papa. Papa was born July 28, 1916 and died June 9, 2001.

I'm so thankful for the memories I have with Papa – fishing together, sitting on the front porch just talking, seeing him walk with his cane. I can't describe what he meant to me, other than to say when he died it was as if someone had cut out a piece of my heart. A part of me was gone. Life just wasn't the same after Papa died.

Nearly seven years later, at the age of 90, Nanny left this world to go be with Papa. She was laid to rest right next to him.

Nanny was one of my best friends. I could always get the scoop on whatever was happening with the family from Nanny. Besides, the two of us could sit on the porch and talk about things all day long without missing a beat. Or not talk… and simply be together.

I had the blessing of hanging out with Nanny for more than 20 years. And every time I saw her, she gave me a kiss on the cheek. You might think this is a trivial thing, but I sure don't. You see, that's exactly how she kissed her biological grandchildren. So that simple gesture told me what she thought of me.

(After Nanny passed, Aunt Athelia organized a family reunion in Destin, Florida. The first year was just a simple vacation to see how we liked it. And man, we all loved it! So now it's an annual event.)

This next tragedy concerns Malis who is, by blood, my Cambodian cousin. But in my heart, she is my sister. Malis has always been there for me.

Some years after her first husband passed, she dated an Egyptian named Fouad. Fouad was about 20 years older than me, but his heart was full of love and respect. Fouad and I, along with our group of friends, loved being together. Whenever there was a cookout or get together, we were all part of it, even those occasional *guy trips* to the casinos at Biloxi. And Fouad was always the life of the party.

Then in 2011, out of the blue, Malis called to tell me he had passed. I was as shocked as she was. He seemed so healthy – in shape, and even athletic – especially for a 50-year-old man. I was devasted and even confused as to why the Lord took away another important person in my life.

Then a little over two years later, on December 13, 2013, my best friend Victor died at the age of 43. Sadly, his death was not that surprising. He never got over his divorce. For the next ten years he just wasn't himself. Victor's death left another big hole, as he played a huge role in my life. I will always regret I didn't have the chance to be with him more during his last days here.

As so often before, I was unprepared for this next tragedy. In fact, this loss was the catalyst that caused me to decide it was now time to write this book.

2018 was a tough flu season in the U.S. On January 11 of that year my business partner, mentor, and one of my dearest, closest friends – Armando Durazo – succumbed to the flu.

Armando was my rock. We talked on a weekly basis. Almost every Friday on my way home from work I checked in with him about our shared business venture. The last time I talked to him he told me that he'd just gotten over a cold he caught while traveling. He sounded a little under the weather, but otherwise fine. And the next thing I know, he's gone. There are times I still can't believe it.

Losing a number of people who were dear to me – and several so unexpectedly – got me thinking a lot more about where I came from and about how I got where I am.

I wanted to know more about my own history. I wanted to learn more about my *original* family – my father and mother and all my siblings. I wanted to understand how my family lived before the war, before I was born.

One day it dawned on me that I knew nothing about myself except that I was from Cambodia and that the Khmer Rouge directly or indirectly murdered my father, my mother, and all but two of my siblings. No one in my Cambodian family ever talked to me about my history or where I came from.

And frankly, up until recently, I was content to be in the dark. But now that I'm older, now that I have children of my own, I do want to know. And I want Christina and my sons to know.

Because to me, the worst of all tragedies – even worse than death itself – is to have lived without purpose and meaning, and to die without understanding your legacy… and without building into that legacy with your own life.

That is not the tragedy I want to be associated with my passing. So this is why I now feel an urgency to know… and tell… my story.

Triumph

When I think of the word "triumph," I see someone who has overcome challenges and setbacks, difficulties and hurdles, and still manages to *rise above*. I see someone who struggled and failed, but who kept getting back up and back in the race until they reached their goal and accomplished what they wanted to accomplish. I can identify with such a person.

I have many goals that I've not yet achieved. But there are many more that have now been moved to the *accomplishments* column.

But I always believed I could do something more, something out of the ordinary. And I wanted to! I wanted to accomplish something brand new like discovering a better way to _____. Maybe it goes back to a childhood spent in a place where every minute you could well say *there's got to be a better way*.

You may remember that it was my Aunt Athelia who initiated our ritual family reunions in Destin, Florida. And each year, at least for a while, the number of people in the family kept growing. One particular year Peter and Chrissy had a baby, JJ and his wife had two, and Christina and I had twins. We rented a house on the beach and everyone piled in. It reminded me of the close-quarters living we had back in Cambodia. I felt right at home!

From the outset Aunt Athelia made certain things very clear. She had rules – a good many of them, in fact – that we were to follow in order to keep her happy and make our time together most enjoyable (enjoyable for her, at any rate).

One such rule was *no diapers in the trash can in the house.*

"Well," [*shit*, I wanted to add – pun intended], "where do you want me to take them?"

"Outside!" she said, with quite a determined look on her face. "Bag them up and throw them outside in the trash!"

It's cold outside in December. But that's evidently beside the point.

So night comes, and nature calls for one of the babies. I get up, change his diaper, find a bag to put it in, and proceed to take the *poop parcel* outside. Once I get back in bed, it takes about an hour or so to fall back to sleep. And then, like clockwork, an hour later the other baby decides to go. Another poop parcel.

Most parents, after changing a diaper, just wait until morning and then dispose of it. But not only did I want to keep Aunt Athelia happy, I also have a nose that is highly sensitive to odors. So even when we're at home with our own rules and I wait until morning, I inevitably smell that brown treasure all night long.

This particular trip starts me thinking that there's got to be a better way to solve this problem. And that thought triggers a process in my mind. The whole time we're in Destin I'm working on this problem in my head, off and on.

And then we head home.

We drive at night so the twins can sleep for the entire trip. But if you've had kids you know that doesn't mean you don't have to stop and change some diapers along the way. And when you do, you live with that odor until you find a lighted rest area or gas station. Unfortunately, the route from Destin to Atlanta is not all highway; it could be miles before you find a suitable rest area.

There's got to be a better way.

Once those gears in my head start turning, there's no stopping them until I find the solution. And voilà… a few months later, I come up with an idea: *"DiaperPods"* – packaging diapers with accompanying bags to put them in.

I take the idea to Peter and ask him what he thinks. He says, "It's a good idea, but people are not going to bite as long as those two things are separate items. There's no intrigue to that. They want to buy a 'pod' technology – an all-in-one solution."

He has a point. Not only that, I am still concerned with the safety of a collection of plastic bags around small children. Safety has to be my top priority.

So I go back to the drawing board.

I buy many different types of diapers, and I test the idea in many ways. After a few more months, I happen to get up in the middle of the night to use the bathroom. To avoid the brightness, I don't typically turn on the lights. But this time I do, and my eyes land on a box of feminine pads, of all things.

I get curious, reach over and grab one and look it over. I notice it is actually encased in a pod. I tear it open and all of a sudden that light bulb in my head comes on.

Since there is no way now I can go back to sleep, I go downstairs and work the rest of the night making a makeshift pod – only this time, with a whole different design.

I show my idea to my friends, and they like it. Then I have Armando over and tell him about it. He isn't impressed… at first. But we keep talking and at some point, his eyes light up.

"You know, you can put this on *any* disposable object. Any object that fits, that is. Forget about diapers," he says. "*Pods* is what we're inventing."

Armando is an investor, you see.

"I want you to help me get this off the ground. I want you to invest in it – *if you believe in it.* Of course, at the same time I don't want you to if you don't." And I meant that.

He said he would give it some thought. And about a week later I get a call from him… "I believe! I believe!"

So in 2009, my friend Armando also became my business partner. Without him, I would not have patented the idea.

We are now patent-protected in the U.S. and Japan. We are awaiting approval in Europe, Canada, and South Korea.

With *DiaperPods* patented, and this book published, there's one more goal I want to accomplish – one more triumph – before I feel like I can honestly say I have earned my way, that I've *given back*.

That goal is to start a nonprofit organization that helps people in a big way. I don't yet know what need it will fill, what it will look like, or how big it will be. But that one is still on my *to-do* list.

Finally, here's a little bit more about yours truly. Just random stuff…
What I love:
- Travel and adventure
- Architectural design of houses, business buildings, and historic constructions (pyramids, temples, etc.)
- The ocean, fishing, and golf
- A cabin in the woods surrounded by mountains
- Cooking for people and making them happy with the gift of good food
- Cleaning – it's relaxing and the results are rewarding
- Fixing things and making them work better
- Laughing and bringing others laughter

What I wish for:
- To fly in a fighter jet, like an F16
- To see a lot more of the world than I have to this point
- To find out what my biological mom and dad, brothers and sisters looked like
- To meet my wife's needs in our relationship
- To watch my kids grow up successfully at whatever worthy endeavor they want to do

Conclusion

When the idea first dropped into my mind to write my story, I dismissed it immediately. At that point in life I was only interested in moving forward to a promising future and further away from a painful past. So I surrounded myself with friends… and as much activity as I could pack in.

But forgetting one's past is not as easy as you might think. The older I got, the less I wanted to keep myself busy… which means I had more time to think. And the more time I had to think, the more I found myself getting sucked back into the vortex of my past.

And now that I have reopened this wound, I realize that *hate* is not what I want to feel. At least for me, the only way to heal is to speak up and speak out.

Remaining quiet about the atrocities that my family and so many others suffered would be accepting that reality as fate. It would be equivalent to standing by and allowing them to have suffered for nothing. That is an unacceptable outcome and one I am not willing to allow.

Once I decided to put my story to print, I expected to end it at the point at which we arrived in America. But as good as America is compared to what we left behind, being a refugee comes with its own set of difficulties.

There were adjustments of adapting to a different culture, learning the language, and dealing with peer criticism and rejection.

Also, for a kid, it was hard to move into a different house in a different neighborhood and attend a different school every year. As soon as I made new friends, I had to leave them and start all over again.

And my frustrations didn't end with childhood. As an adult I grew tired of moving from one job to another. It seemed I was always being forced to change, forced to try again, all the while feeling like I really didn't fit in and would never be fully accepted by some people.

So by the time I landed in the hospital after having nearly bled to death from my ulcer, I was sick of it all – more than I can describe.

If you've ever been in a similar place in life, you understand. And if you are there now, I want you to take hope from my journey.

Today is a new day, my friend. If you will just open yourself up to possibilities, you will find they are everywhere.

The truth is that I was blessed in Cambodia, and I have been blessed in America. I have no idea where I would be without the *countless* people who risked their lives and went above and beyond to help me all along the way.

In this book, and with good reason, I have referred to them as my heroes.

Because of them, I now consider myself richer than Croesus – and in many ways more successful. I believe that being rich includes the ability to appreciate what you have and make the most out of the life you've been given… and pursuing the opportunity to give back every chance you get.

This is why my cousin, Annette, and I chose – after a visit to Cambodia a few years back – to sponsor a man and his three kids (two boys and one girl). At that time, the boys were around nine or ten years old and the girl was about seven.

They still live just a few miles from my house, and the kids are now grown. As a matter of fact, the girl is in nursing school and the two boys are working in a manufacturing company and going to college.

They are on a similar path to my own, and I pray that a Higher Power will continue to guide their way and help them live good lives so they, in turn, may also begin to give back.

All the children who – along with me, my siblings, and my cousins – survived the Cambodian genocide, are now in their 30s and 40s. Some are doctors, others are lawyers, dancers, writers, singers, movie directors, business owners, or otherwise simply decent people making their own contribution to society just like natural-born Americans.

I smile when I consider the paths they traveled and the strengths they possess. I know like me, they appreciate life in America and the opportunities that abound here.

If I could sum up America in one word, it would be this: *potential.*

I live my life owing to this priceless gift of opportunity. We refugees, you see, do not typically take our freedom and opportunities for granted.

To those who gave us that second chance, *thank you!* To those who are committed to diversity, inclusion, and equality, and to those who can look beyond the color of skin and see that it's the person's character that matters, *thank you!* To those who do not tolerate discrimination based on religion and national origin, *thank you!*

And to those who embrace humanity as I do, let us raise a glass! Let us be grateful together for not only the opportunity – but also the *responsibility* – we each have to be *great*, to live well, and to give back.

God bless you!

Ung Family Timeline

Until late 1970 – Takeo Province

1971 to 1973 – Phnom Penh

1973 to 1975 – Battambang

1975 to 1981 – Forced into the countryside to live in various workcamps and refugee camps

1981 – Sponsorship to America

Made in the USA
Coppell, TX
24 November 2021

66347927R00122